Letter to the

Dear Reader,

After having been a wedding planner and floral designer for twenty-three years in the Washington, DC, metropolitan area (along with planning weddings in over thirty countries as a destination wedding planner), there has been nothing like writing this book during the COVID-19 pandemic. My perspective in the midst of planning and executing micro weddings during the pandemic has been a unique one for sure.

My underlying reason for writing this book had everything to do with watching couples compromise over the years due to societal and family pressures along with outdated etiquette rules that simply don't apply to the modern couple.

I love the fact that a micro wedding allows a couple to really focus on what *they* want for their wedding day. Micro weddings work for any budget and style and are also much easier on the environment than traditional large-scale events. Sustainable, stylish, and meaningful weddings have always been part of my core mission as a wedding designer. A micro wedding is perfect for any couple who truly wants to celebrate their love with the people they love! I am honored that you have chosen my book as your wedding planning guide.

Congratulations and Happy Planning!

Katie Martin

Welcome to the Everything® Series!

These handy, accessible books give you all you need to tackle a difficult project, gain a new hobby, comprehend a fascinating topic, prepare for an exam, or even brush up on something you learned back in school but have since forgotten.

You can choose to read an Everything® book from cover to cover or just pick out the information you want from our four useful boxes: Questions, Facts, Alerts, and Essentials. We give you everything you need to know on the subject, but throw in a lot of fun stuff along the way too.

question	fact
Answers to common questions.	Important snippets of information.

alert	essential
Urgent warnings.	Quick handy tips.

We now have more than 600 Everything® books in print, spanning such wide-ranging categories as cooking, health, parenting, personal finance, wedding planning, word puzzles, and so much more. When you're done reading them all, you can finally say you know Everything®!

PUBLISHER Karen Cooper

MANAGING EDITOR Lisa Laing

COPY CHIEF Casey Ebert

PRODUCTION EDITOR Jo-Anne Duhamel

ACQUISITIONS EDITOR Rebecca Tarr Thomas

DEVELOPMENT EDITOR Sarah Doughty

EVERYTHING® SERIES COVER DESIGNER Erin Alexander

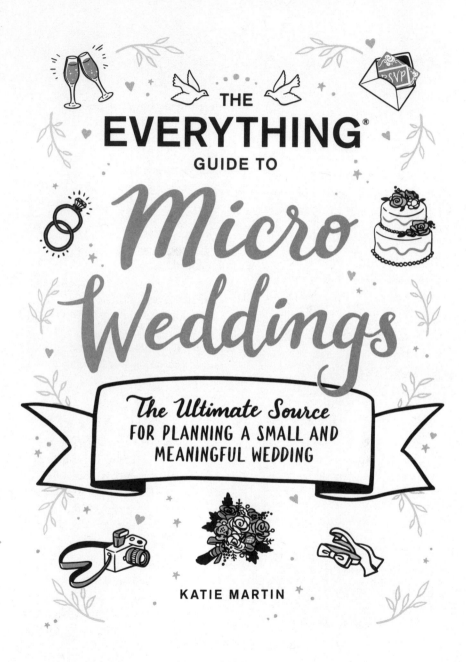

THE EVERYTHING® GUIDE TO

Micro Weddings

The Ultimate Source FOR PLANNING A SMALL AND MEANINGFUL WEDDING

KATIE MARTIN

Adams Media

New York London Toronto Sydney New Delhi

Adams Media
An Imprint of Simon & Schuster, Inc.
100 Technology Center Drive
Stoughton, Massachusetts 02072

An Everything® Series Book. Everything®
and everything.com® are registered
trademarks of Simon & Schuster, Inc.

First Adams Media trade paperback
edition October 2021

ADAMS MEDIA and colophon are
trademarks of Simon & Schuster.

For information about special discounts
for bulk purchases, please contact Simon &
Schuster Special Sales at 1-866-506-1949
or business@simonandschuster.com.

The Simon & Schuster Speakers Bureau
can bring authors to your live event. For
more information or to book an event
contact the Simon & Schuster Speakers
Bureau at 1-866-248-3049 or visit our
website at www.simonspeakers.com.

Interior design by Colleen Cunningham
and Julia Jacintho
Illustrations and hand lettering by
Priscilla Yuen

Manufactured in the
United States of America

1 2021

Library of Congress Cataloging-in-
Publication Data
Names: Martin, Katie, 1972– author.
Title: The everything® guide to micro
weddings / Katie Martin.
Description: Stoughton, Massachusetts:
Adams Media, 2021 | Series: Everything®
series | Includes index.
Identifiers: LCCN 2021021480 |
ISBN 9781507216200 (pb) | ISBN
9781507216217 (ebook)
Subjects: LCSH: Weddings--Planning. |
Marriage service--Planning.
Classification: LCC HQ745 .M3246 2021
| DDC 392.5--dc23
LC record available at
https://lccn.loc.gov/2021021480

ISBN 978-1-5072-1620-0
ISBN 978-1-5072-1621-7

Contains material adapted from the
following title published by Adams Media,
an Imprint of Simon & Schuster, Inc.: The
Everything® Wedding Book, 5th Edition by
Katie Martin, copyright © 2014, ISBN
978-1-4405-6958-6.

For Miguel, Derek, and Elena.
¡Los quiero mucho mucho mucho!

This book is dedicated to all my clients and
vendors who hired me and worked alongside me
during the COVID-19 pandemic. Those weddings gave
me endless inspiration for this book and helped forge friendships and loyalty that I will be forever grateful for.

Contents

Acknowledgments

I must start by thanking my incredible husband, Miguel. Te amo, cariño! I will always be thankful for my two children, Derek and Elena, as they motivate and encourage me daily. Special thanks to my mom (my personal cheerleader).

I am forever grateful for my clients and vendor colleagues for being the source of my creativity and inspiration.

Thanks to everyone at Simon & Schuster, Inc. who has helped make this book become a reality and a resource for engaged couples and their families. Special thanks to Rachel, Lisa, and Sarah for guiding me throughout the process.

Introduction

Are you set on having a smaller wedding with a more intimate feel? Looking to save money *without* sacrificing any of the elements you want at your event? Hoping to showcase your unique style through the reception décor?

The increasingly popular micro wedding can provide a truly special experience for you and your partner (and your guests!). Whether you're hoping to cut costs, stay safe, reduce your environmental impact, or customize the décor to your specific interests, a smaller event allows you to focus on the people and things you truly want for an unforgettable day that doesn't sacrifice any of your desires.

Of course, micro weddings still involve a lot of exciting choices, as well as special opportunities for adding personal touches. With *The Everything® Guide to Micro Weddings*, you will be able to explore each important element of planning a micro wedding and determine the decorations, food and beverage items, reception setting, and more that will help you create a wedding that is unique to you and your partner. If you are imagining a destination micro wedding getaway, this book will show you the best places to go. Wanting something closer to home? There are tips and how-tos for that as well. You'll explore insights and important considerations for every element of your big day, from flowers and lighting to catering and photography. You'll also find an Appendix with checklists to help stay organized through it all.

A wedding should be a day full of love, romance, and fun! A micro wedding is about the two of you getting married the way *you* want to, without necessarily following all of society and wedding "rules." After reading this book, you should be able to get excited about your day while focusing on a shorter guest list, realistic budget, and your unique tastes! Enjoy looking through photos and search engines. Take your time on social media apps to dream about your micro wedding day and share ideas with your family and friends. This book will help you determine, organize, and execute what is right for your day, your way—no sacrifices necessary. Have fun, revel, and celebrate having one of the most meaningful and stylish days of your life: your wedding!

Chapter One

Why Have a Micro Wedding?

So you are engaged and ready to plan your wedding. Maybe you've always been interested in keeping things small and intimate, or you've just recently heard about the increasingly popular wedding trend: micro weddings. Regardless of what has drawn you to learn more, this chapter has answers to all your questions and provides inspiration for a day that is unique to you and your partner. In the following pages, you'll explore the basics of a micro wedding, from what it is to the five main themes surrounding micro weddings, including personalization and saving money. It's time to start creating your perfect day!

What Is a Micro Wedding?

Simply put, a micro wedding is a wedding with fifty or fewer guests. Most micro weddings are held in smaller spaces, outdoor spots, private homes, or destination cities. More important, micro weddings focus on immediate family members and super-close friends as guests. With a smaller guest list, couples zero in on who they absolutely must share the day with, like a dear childhood friend, and who they can send a simple engagement announcement to if they wish, like Great Aunt Carol's second cousin Jeffrey.

In the next sections, you'll explore the five main reasons why a micro wedding may be the perfect choice for you and your partner. Whether you are looking to save money, skip any traditions that don't fit your needs and style, or even reduce your wedding's carbon footprint, a micro wedding is all about what matters to you on your dream day.

1. You Can Focus On What's Important

Classic "must-haves," the parental guidance, wedding party coordination, mounting expenses, and expanding guest lists—the traditional big wedding comes with so much to consider (and so many opportunities for headaches), and not all of it is what the engaged couple actually *wants*. But there's another way! With micro weddings, these stressors can be greatly reduced, if not eliminated.

A micro wedding emphasizes what matters most to a couple versus how they might please everyone else. While there is *nothing* wrong with a large and glam wedding, smaller events create more space to focus on close friends, family, and the couple themselves. And on one of the most important days of your life, it makes sense to concentrate more on the right people than how big your wedding can be.

2. You Can Personalize Your Wedding

Over the years, weddings have gotten more and more creative. The countless options available for unique venues, food and beverages, guest activities, interactive social media elements, and more make it possible to tailor your wedding any way you want. Looking to showcase you and your partner's love for all things sweet? You can include a dessert buffet as the focal point of your reception venue. And why not jump on whatever is trending in the culinary wedding world, like a doughnut wall or make-your-own-sundae station? Hoping to bring something reminiscent of your childhood to the big day? Bounce houses in every size, color, and theme are available to make the event memorable. Instead of a classic photo booth, you can also ramp up the nostalgia with a caricature station.

A micro wedding is all about personalization and making sure that the couple is the focus. It's their day, and everything from the color scheme to the hors d'oeuvres should reflect that! The main ways to personalize a micro wedding are food, fashion, and décor. In the next sections, you'll explore each of these elements in more detail.

Food

Having hors d'oeuvres, entrées, snacks, and desserts that truly reflect the tastes of a couple is a great way to personalize the experience. In keeping with the intimate feel in most micro weddings, many incorporate fun personal or local themes like beloved family recipes and vendors that offer foods popular to the region. There may be pre-ceremony charcuterie boards or customized cocktails, along with late-night snacks that reflect the couple's inner foodie. Food is part of the fun when it comes to planning a micro wedding, so be sure to pick the right restaurant or caterer that resonates with your vision for the day (and your tastebuds!).

Fashion

You may have attended or heard of micro weddings in which couples ditch the standard wedding garb for a different style of dress or jumpsuit for the bride(s) and comfortable suit or more casual clothing for the groom(s). Since a small wedding is focused more on the intimacy of the event and less on things being "matchy-matchy," the attire you select for you, your partner, and your wedding party is completely unlimited.

> **fact**
>
> Does a red jumpsuit feel more "you" than a white or ivory dress? Wear whatever speaks to who you are. Because micro weddings are made up of only close friends and family members, everyone at your wedding will understand the choice. Your style will shine through more brightly if you wear what you love!

While you can be color coordinated, take a hint from the venue, the season you are getting married in, or even the color palette of your life (the clothes you buy and furnishings in your home and office) to determine the hues that feel right for your event. You can also let your wedding party pick from a few different colors or a color palette rather than giving them a set outfit to wear. In terms of your guests, they can also become part of the style of the day if you clue them in to the theme ahead of time. Why not? Style your wedding the way you want to, within your budget and without all the stuffy rules!

Décor

Many micro weddings have décor that reflects the interests and passions of the couple. Since less money is spent on food, beverages, and wedding attendants (people in the wedding party) at micro weddings, you may have more room to incorporate exactly what you want, whether it's an elaborate ice sculpture or more fresh flower accents. When planning your décor, you can usually increase your budget from the average 7 percent to 10 percent for a traditional wedding to 10 percent to 15 percent for a micro wedding.

There are five ways to really personalize your day with décor:

1. **Backdrops.** Since the dawn of social media, backdrops (curtains, wooden and metal frames, floral walls, etc.) have become a focal point at many events. A backdrop for a ceremony can be reused as a backdrop for guests to take photos in front of to post on *Instagram*, *Facebook*, and TikTok, for example. Many couples create backdrops that can be reused after their wedding as well, like a wooden frame fitted with lights that can be repurposed as décor for your backyard.

> **essential**
>
> Get the biggest bang for your buck when it comes to backdrops. Many couples opt for interesting signage (like laser-cut lettering or neon signs). Neon signs are an excellent investment as they can last a lifetime and provide a beautiful daily reminder of your wedding day!

When planning a wedding, backdrops are usually on the more expensive end, but may easily fit into your micro wedding budget. Décor vendors can create a backdrop that works for your ceremony and can be quickly transformed or added to as a photo backdrop during the reception.

2. **Flowers.** Here is where you can really have the flowers you have always dreamed of. If your wedding is in June and you love peonies—perfect! While peonies can be expensive, you won't need a ton, as a micro wedding means fewer attendants who will need bouquets or boutonnières and tables that will need centerpieces. Flowers can add décor to entrances, bathrooms, open bars, and so on. Instead of scrimping on the minimum décor for a three-hundred-guest wedding, a micro wedding lets you have all the flowers (and other elements) you want!

3. **Plant Rentals.** People love plants! Plant rentals are one way to fill up empty spaces and give a room a cozier feel—which can be crucial for a micro wedding in a medium-sized or larger venue. Some of the best plants to use to fill space and help give a cozier feel to your micro wedding are ficus trees, areca palm trees, fiddle leaf fig trees, arboricolas, Boston ferns, rubber trees, and monstera plants. Plants can become your "best friend," closing the gap where flowers and other types of décor can't (not to mention they are super cost-effective).

4. **Furniture.** You can change the feel of any venue with furniture. Instead of those heinous-looking conference chairs at your venue, bring in gorgeous rental furniture vignettes, classic wooden benches, or upholstered vintage chairs to create the look you want. Some furniture rental companies provide rustic, romantic, and vintage-chic styles, while others focus on more modern luxury and clean lines.

5. **Lighting.** Any event designer will tell you that lighting changes everything. For a nighttime wedding or venue with limited natural light, lighting is essential to creating atmosphere. Amber lighting is the most popular for weddings as it helps people look younger in photos! However, other options such as bistro lighting can create wonderful

ambiance. You can also use lit logos, pin spot lighting, and more. Keep in mind that lighting can be costly, so you will want to investigate different options and figure out where this element fits into your budget.

> **fact**
>
> Did you know that amber and soft glow lighting started in the 1970s with TV celebrities wanting to look younger? It worked—and stuck. You can get the same celebrity treatment by using amber and/or soft glow lighting for your micro wedding!

3. You'll Save Money

Saving money is the number one concern of most couples while planning their weddings. Luckily, there is no doubt that a micro wedding will give you more control over your budget. Saving money happens automatically when you reduce your guest count, but there are many other ways that you can cut costs along the way without sacrificing anything you really want on your perfect day.

Hors D'oeuvres

At most weddings, the cocktail hour gives everyone a chance to grab a drink and some hors d'oeuvres and get to know other guests. With a reduced guest count, the caterers need less time to feed everyone, less food and alcohol, and fewer servers—all of which mean less money spent by the couple. This also leads many couples to reduce their cocktail hour to less than sixty minutes. This free time is often filtered into the time allotted for post-ceremony photos, or another activity a couple might feel is more important than the cocktail hour.

Dinner

Some couples are particularly excited about the food element of their wedding and want a big, long dinner. They may cut or shorten the cocktail hour and/or other post-ceremony events to leave more time and room in the budget for a lengthier, larger meal. But if you want to get to the party and dancing part of the reception quickly, you may opt for a cocktail-style reception, greatly reducing the amount of food needed. Cocktail-style food usually means smaller portions with a larger variety of food. Caterers have become uniquely positioned to create interesting experiences for micro weddings through fun, interactive food stations that can be set up and closed down as quickly as a couple chooses. And gone are the days of your standard protein, starch, and vegetable dinner: Micro weddings can have anything from individual charcuterie boards and multiple courses paired with different wines to more laid-back options like barbecue or pizza—whatever reflects the personality and style of the couple!

> **alert**
>
> When it comes to serving family-style dinners, it's important to be careful. For health reasons such as allergies or intolerances, some guests may not feel comfortable with community food platters. Instead, ask your caterer for French service (where servers bring out beautiful platters and serve each guest their choices from these platters) with gloved servers to better serve your guests with safety in mind.

If you are a vegan or vegetarian, serving a meal free of meat or animal by-products is another easy way to save money, as plant-based menus are almost always less expensive than menus with meat products. Whatever your style, always ask your caterers for cost-effective ways to help manage your budget. You'll explore planning the food for your micro wedding in Chapter 7.

Desserts

Wedding cakes have become incredible works of art. And art costs. After all, there is an enormous amount of talent and time involved in creating the delicious masterpieces that you may have seen all over *Pinterest* and *Instagram*. However, not everyone likes cake. Many couples are opting for more cost-effective desserts that better match their tastes and personality. For example, if you and your partner love going out for ice cream each Sunday, why not have an ice cream bar with a small cutting cake? If you like cookies, take a cue from Ohio and Western Pennsylvania and have all your guests bring their finest batch of a dozen cookies for everyone to choose from. With fifty guests, that is a *lot* of free cookies!

> **alert**
>
> If you're bringing in your own food to the reception, be sure to consult with your venue and caterer to make sure that food-handling safety will be adhered to and whether there are any rules about bringing in outside food. You don't want any surprises on the big day.

No matter what you imagine for the dessert portion of your evening, you can save a lot of money in this department. See Chapter 10 for more DIY ideas for desserts.

Beverages

Alcohol is a major cost for a wedding, and something that is often overlooked during the planning process. Many caterers offer alcohol, but this can be pricey, as you are paying for their logistics and expertise along with the alcohol itself. To save as much money as possible, book a venue that allows you to bring in your own alcohol. Of course, in addition to buying the alcohol, you'll need to plan the logistics of it. Be sure to ask someone trustworthy to be in charge of dropping the alcohol off at the venue either the day before or early the day of the wedding.

---

essential

Now that it is becoming more widely acceptable for people to abstain from alcohol at weddings, consider having a few mocktail options for your guests. Mocktails with accents like chipotle and ginger for a punch or fun candy and fruit flavors creates a celebratory atmosphere welcoming of guests' personal preferences.

Ask your caterer beforehand for their recommendations on the types of wine needed to pair with the food being served, but when it comes to everything else beverage-wise, keep it light! The cheapest route is to serve beer and wine and no mixed drinks. If you like mixed drinks, keep it to only one or two signature cocktails during cocktail hour only. You don't have to spend money for a champagne toast, either, as people can toast with what they have in hand. Don't forget that you will need to take all your leftover alcohol at the end of the night if you are providing it. Be sure to ask someone to take the items to your home or return the unopened or unchilled inventory back to where it was purchased, especially if you are going on a honeymoon right after the wedding (more on this in Chapter 7).

Décor and Flowers

When it comes to décor and flowers for micro weddings, the smaller guest count will automatically save you money on tables, chairs, linens, and tabletop items (such as plates, glassware, and flatware). Having fewer tables and guests means fewer floral centerpieces. And fewer people in your wedding party means fewer flowers for bridesmaids or groomsmen as well. Don't be fooled, though: Some flowers cost way more than others. For example, peonies and ranunculus are expensive for two very different reasons: Peonies are normally only available during May and June and are always in high demand, while ranunculus bloom in small amounts that add up in cost depending on how much of the flower you want. Garden roses are extremely delicate and are always going to be more expensive than regular cut roses.

Here are a few questions that are important to ask when meeting with a potential florist for your wedding day:

- Do you have a price minimum?
- Can you work within my budget? (Wedding designers are used to being creative, and many will have ideas on how to save money if your budget is limited.)
- What forms of payment do you accept?

Venue

Since micro weddings have a smaller number of guests (an average of thirty-five), there is a huge range in pricing in terms of where to have your wedding. Smaller weddings mean more choices—and more possibilities for inexpensive or even free locations. You can have your wedding at your apartment, your church or temple, mom's house, a local park, an interesting memorial, a public historical location, a hiking trail, the beach, a small restaurant—the list goes on!

The more expensive options will still typically be more cost-effective, as you will be renting a smaller space and will need fewer tables, chairs, etc. (in the case of a venue that provides these items). International resorts can also be more cost-effective, as they are usually all-inclusive and may even offer perks such as a wedding cake or basic reception package as part of the total cost.

fact

When planning your micro wedding, keep an interesting destination as a possibility. Many international wedding destinations have incredible packages to save you money while including lodging and excursions for you and your guests. Learn more about this in Chapter 4.

Wedding Clothing

With a micro wedding, anything goes! You don't even have to get a new dress or a new suit for the occasion if you don't want to. You make the rules. If you want to wear your favorite blue dress or khakis, why not? Wear what you love, and save a lot of money at the same time! You can also make the fashion styling rules more relaxed for anyone who will be in your wedding party so they can wear an affordable dress or suit they love as well and can wear again and again.

essential

Let vendors know your budget. If they can't stay within your budget, the selection process gets easier for you. Wedding vendors are not car dealers with millions of dollars in advertising. Most of them are small business owners and really want the referrals and photos after your event, so it behooves them to work within your budget if they are able!

As micro weddings have grown more popular, the wedding industry has seen shorter gowns, sexier details, dresses in different colors, and suits that range from tuxes to shorts. Be sure to set the tone for your style choices by letting guests and your vendors know the formality level of your wedding as well. Make wedding planning fun and stress-free by going along with your fashion sense and budget—everyone else is sure to play along!

4. You Can Help the Environment

At the turn of the twenty-first century, a major shift began around the world to focus on global warming and climate change—and this shift has affected every single industry. The wedding industry embraced the idea of "green" weddings at the beginning of the twenty-first century, but early versions simply featured the color green with accents of burlap. It took a while, but after years of reinventing the trend, various wedding planners, gown designers, and wedding vendors were able to showcase truly sustainable wedding designs that had nothing to do with the color green (or burlap, for that matter).

When the micro wedding trend started to gain popularity in 2017, more and more interesting eco-friendly aspects of weddings became widely accepted and used in the planning process. The very essence of a micro wedding being smaller and more intimate makes it more sustainable in a few key ways.

Less Food Waste

The number one issue with sustainability when it comes to weddings is food waste. Most caterers will tell you that once the guest list tops fifty, the amount of waste increases substantially. Caterers almost always have to bring extra food to weddings to be prepared for last-minute allergies and food choice preferences, and many guests simply may not finish their meal or eat the amount of hors d'oeuvres that were budgeted. Fewer guests means less food wasted. You can also ask your caterer to recycle all plastic and metal containers (especially at the bar) and use a compost service for the food waste produced by the event. All of this is very easy to do and cost-effective. You should also ask your caterer to use as many local purveyors (food markets, vendors, etc.) as possible.

Smaller Wedding Parties

In larger, more traditional weddings, bridesmaids are typically forced to buy a dress they will never wear again. You might adore that rich deep shade of purple while your bestie hates it. Why put them through that? Having a smaller wedding party means the opportunity to give your bridesmaids and groomsmen choices in what they wear. You can steer them in a color palette direction but letting them choose an outfit that they will truly love makes a difference in their pocket and closet! It also helps your attendants feel more relaxed and confident.

Less Transportation

This is a big one. A micro wedding means fewer people needing transportation. Fewer cars traveling to your wedding venue(s) means less carbon emissions (unless all of your guests are arriving in energy-efficient and electric-powered vehicles, which would be surprising and impressive). You will also possibly have fewer vendors and catering staff, which again will result in less transportation needed. And finally, when it comes to transporting your wedding party, the fewer vehicles needed, the lesser your carbon footprint.

Sustainable Favors

Most micro weddings have done away with the standard plastic-wrapped favors that will never be used by your guests. Instead, many couples opt for welcome bags and kits to help guests enjoy their time at the wedding. For example, a wedding welcome canvas bag with a refillable water bottle and locally made snacks is always a hit. This provides guests with a bag to reuse at the grocery store, a water bottle to take them around the wedding locations and then use at home, and items that give back to the local community.

> **fact**
>
> Historically, wedding favors are an invention of the wedding industry to encourage you to spend money. If you find something you love, then buy it for your guests, but nobody is entitled to a wedding favor. Your guests are there for *you*.

Sustainability in weddings in large part depends on how far away your products are purchased and how they are manufactured (travel and logistics always play the biggest part in how environmentally-friendly a wedding is—outside of number of guests). Always be aware of where the different components of your wedding are made. And beyond sustainability, the lower number of favors, welcome bags, or kits you need for your smaller guest list automatically means less potential for waste.

5. You Won't Have to Wait

One of the most interesting parts of the micro wedding is that you typically don't see long waiting times and engagements. Larger budgets and larger guest counts often come with a longer waiting period. The reason for long engagements most of the time has to do with money and, of course, time constraints and commitments with everyone involved with the process. The couple, parental units, extended family, wedding party, guests from in town, guests from out of town, and all their different needs creates a longer planning timeline. Many couples who are planning their micro wedding actually get excited when their list becomes smaller. The more intimate, the easier the planning might be. And when it comes to Save the Dates, you'll have a faster reaction to RSVP requests (especially if you mention your wedding website on your Save the Dates), so you can quickly utilize your "B" and "C" lists of people once you get "no" RSVPs from the "A" list (more on prioritizing your lists in Chapter 3). You have the exact number of people you want, and all the choices are yours as a couple. With this control and fewer people to factor in, you can set the date that is most convenient for you as opposed to when everyone else is available. If you don't want to wait a year or more to get married, you don't have to!

Chapter Two

The Wedding Date and Tone

Now that you are decided on having a micro wedding, it's time to set the date and the tone of your big day. In this chapter, you'll explore the different considerations for choosing a date, as well as how to tell the world about your engagement and choice to have a micro wedding. As you'll discover, a major component of setting the tone and theme of your wedding is your budget. If this is already making you sweat, don't worry: This chapter also includes everything you need to know about hiring a wedding planner to help reduce wedding planning stress!

Telling Your Families

Once you are engaged, and certainly before you jump into planning your micro wedding, you will want to tell everyone the exciting news! Take special care to tell the most important people in your lives first. The last thing you want to do when announcing this momentous occasion is hurt anyone close to you. While you might think your wedding is a wholly personal thing between you and your betrothed, your immediate family might not think the same way. Weddings are a rite of passage. Some parents take this rite a little more to heart depending on their religion, culture, family ties, or other factors. Your individual relationships with each parent, sibling, and other family members will dictate how you announce your engagement to those people. The following sections explore the whos and hows of announcing your engagement in more depth.

Telling Your Child

The first person who should be told about your upcoming nuptials is your child or children, if you have any. Whether this is your first wedding or not, your child has the right to know before anyone else does. Your marriage will affect them more than anyone else in your family.

> **essential**
>
> Depending on the age of your child, you should consider enlisting the help of a therapist or counselor to talk to them about your engagement. If you have a younger child who is dealing with a divorce or the death of a parent, a therapist or counselor will help you navigate the potentially difficult news of your impending marriage.

Hopefully, you have prepared your child for the possibility of your engagement. If you have not prepared them, there are two things you will need to communicate to your child now that you are engaged. The first and most important thing is that you are not trying to replace a parent. The second thing is how your lives will change in positive ways both during the planning process and after the wedding. Also keep in mind that each child is different: You and your fiancé will want to spend time planning this conversation in advance, depending on the age(s) of your child/children and their mental preparedness for this event.

Telling Your Parents

If possible, it is always recommended to announce your engagement to your parents in person. If both sets of parents are far away from you (and each other), try to set up a weekend for them to share the news and allow them to get to know each other if they don't already.

> **question**
>
> **What should I do if my parents are divorced or remarried?**
> Try your best to inform all parents on the same day. "Traditional" etiquette calls for telling the parents of the bride first followed by the groom's parents. Be sure to speak to your parents directly and not through a stepparent.

If having your parents meet each other is too difficult to do before the week of your wedding, make plans for a special meeting before your rehearsal, or try a virtual online meeting. The last thing you want to do is have your parents meet for the first time on your actual wedding day. Your parents love you and will want to know at least a little bit about the family you are marrying into before the wedding day itself. Meeting each other prior to the wedding will help make the wedding day more comfortable and fun for both sets of parents.

Telling Your Former Spouse

If you have a former spouse, it is always best for you to be the first person to inform them. Do not send the information about your engagement through someone else, especially not through a mutual child. If there is no child involved and/or communication is difficult, an email or handwritten note is sufficient. Be prepared for renewed discussions of alimony and child support (if there are any children). Consult with your attorney before discussing these issues with your former spouse.

> **fact**
>
> The issue of a former spouse can be a source of great difficulty for a couple planning their wedding. The best course to take is to be open and honest with your fiancé and both of your immediate families. After discussing the possibilities, you should be able to decide what is best for all involved.

Of course, if you feel your former spouse is the type to try and disrupt your wedding, you can choose not to disclose any wedding details to them. In this case, make sure family and mutual friends don't reveal information, either, and refrain from newspaper announcements until after the wedding.

Telling Your Late Spouse's Family

If either you or your fiancé were married before to a person who is now deceased, news of your upcoming remarriage may be difficult for the late spouse's family. Depending on how close you are to them, you may choose to tell them in person or in a tactful handwritten note. Whatever you choose, make sure it is you who tells them. Do not let them hear it through the grapevine or after the wedding.

Announcing Your Micro Wedding

Once you've announced your engagement, you can start spreading the great news. Announcing a micro wedding is no different from announcing any other wedding. With today's technology and creative media, you have several ways of sharing the excitement.

The traditional way of letting the world know about your upcoming nuptials is, of course, through the local newspaper. With the advent of social media, fewer people read actual hard-copy newspapers, as most people now consume their "newspapers" online. This, however, does not mean that online newspapers don't do announcements; they most certainly do. For traditional weddings, the parents of the bride submit newspaper announcements. This announcement gives general information about the couple, including their schooling, careers, how the couple met, and where the wedding will take place. Many include an official engagement photo.

The announcement information is usually sent to the lifestyle or society editor of the newspaper. Every newspaper is different, so be sure to check out their website or call their administrative offices before you or your parents (or your fiancé's parents) submit a traditional announcement. Some newspapers announce for free and some charge a fee. If you, your parents, and/or your fiancé's parents live in different cities or states, you may decide to submit an announcement to each local paper. In this case, be sure to send each family a copy of the engagement announcement (wording and photo) to pass along.

Another popular way to announce your engagement is through an engagement portrait session. After setting a date, why not look for a photographer right away for your wedding? This way, you can check a vendor off your wedding planning checklist, and you'll have a photographer lined up to take engagement photos as well as photos of any other party you may end up having in addition to the wedding day. After getting the photos back from your engagement session, send an email to the guests you are going to invite. You can also post the photos on all your social media platforms, which does the trick of letting everyone know!

Sharing the Micro Details

Having a small, intimate wedding may not be what your entire family or even close friends are interested in. Following the news of your engagement, you may have to spend time explaining your decision to go smaller and less traditional. Depending on who you are talking to, it may not be an easy sell, and that is okay. At the end of the day, this is your wedding, and those who love you will need to set aside differing opinions to give their support. Check out the section on managing expectations later in this chapter for more information on handling family opinions and disagreements regarding your wedding.

Choosing a Date

Now that the announcements have been made, it's time to get planning! And that starts with a wedding date. There is nothing more important than picking your date—you can't get married, and your guests can't be there to share the occasion with you, without one. Here are questions to help you narrow your search for *the* date:

- Which season(s) do you prefer?
- Do you like snow?
- When and where did you fall in love?
- What kind of food would you like to have served? (This has a lot to do with seasonality and availability of certain foods.)
- What are your favorite colors? (Some colors coincide with certain times of year.)
- Is there a particular time of year that your families find meaningful?
- Do you want an outdoors ceremony and/or reception?
- How much time do you have to plan your wedding?
- Do you prefer the heat or the cold?
- Do you like cities or more rural locations?
- Are there military and other family commitments like pregnancies and home purchases to consider?
- Are there birthdays or holidays you want to avoid or tie into the event?
- What school or work schedules are there to consider?
- Are there any health issues to consider?

The answers to all of these questions play a role in determining the general timing of your wedding. Once you have settled on a season and you have weeded out dates that don't mesh well with all of the familial and wedding party calendars, you will be off to the races. It is important to be as flexible as possible with your date as you start the search for your ceremony and reception sites. Your wedding date and venues are what set the tone for your event, so be careful in your selections, and the rest of the planning process will be much easier.

Depending on where you live, December may be a popular wedding month because of the holiday season. Or February may be because of Valentine's Day. Every city is different, and every couple is different! The key is to be open during this part of the process and do your research. Also account for your families' needs: Remember, the two of you are getting married and entering each other's families! Start off on the right foot with your fiancé's family—you will be grateful you did once the wedding is over.

Happy Holidays?

Should your wedding day be over a long holiday weekend, such as Memorial Day, Labor Day, or Columbus Day/ Indigenous Peoples' Day? Does the sound of a festive holiday season wedding sound incredible to you? What about a New Year's Eve celebration or a romantic Valentine's Day theme? There are pros and cons to each of these ideas.

LONG WEEKEND HOLIDAYS

With a long holiday weekend wedding, there are three major pros. The first is that your guests will appreciate a wedding on a long weekend. It will give them an extra day of rest after the event before they have to travel back home (if they are coming from out of town). Second, you get to celebrate a major holiday with all of your family and friends, and it will give you extra time to do other activities together (like sightseeing, if your wedding is in an interesting city) that are not associated with the wedding. The last fantastic pro to consider is your honeymoon. Having your wedding on a holiday weekend means an extra day for your honeymoon, saving at least one of your precious vacation days from work!

essential

If you live in a major city that celebrates a holiday by holding festivals and other activities, be sure to do your research ahead of time. If you plan your wedding for a holiday weekend, include these activities on your Save the Dates, your wedding website, and wedding invitation information insert card. This is also important to help guests who are planning to travel for the wedding and if you need to factor in possible traffic.

Of course, with pros there are also cons. First and foremost, you will not be the only one who has thought of having a wedding on a long holiday weekend. Along with you will be a long list of other couples wanting the same venues, photographers, and florists for the same date. You will have to make quick decisions. With this in mind, the next con is that you will have less negotiating power with your wedding professionals. It's simple supply and demand. Some wedding professionals may even charge more for these weekends as they end up having to pay their own staff additional wages to work on holidays, so be prepared for a higher price tag. Finally, you will be in competition with long-standing vacation plans that your guests may already have. Both Memorial Day and Labor Day weekends are popular beach getaway and vacation times.

WINTER HOLIDAYS

Weddings during the winter holiday season, in particular, work best for large families that tend to get together for the holidays anyway. However, this means that both sets of families have to be willing to celebrate together. If you are looking for an intimate micro wedding, the winter holiday season could be your best bet. The holidays are generally filled with traditions and spirituality you may want to incorporate into your special day. However, these events can also come with more stress regarding family relationships, money, and more.

> **alert**
>
> At certain times of the year, major religious holidays can affect whether or not some of your guests can attend your wedding. If anyone in your wedding party has strict religious beliefs, be ready to not only check their calendars but their diet and other possible observances.

Another possible con of a winter holiday wedding is that gifts are traditionally given during this season. It may make it harder financially for your guests and wedding party to pay for travel and outfits in addition to all of the gifts they may be planning to purchase. You will want to keep your guests in mind more when it comes to getting married during this season.

The holiday that technically ends the winter holiday season in the United States is New Year's Eve/Day. Many weddings are held on New Year's Eve as it is a great reason to have a party! Your guests will delight in being able to dress to the nines for your wedding day.

Some of the same cons of long weekend and other winter holiday weddings will apply to this holiday. Many wedding professionals charge more for New Year's Eve, and traveling on or around this date can be very hectic, stressful, and costly. Also, many couples see New Year's Eve as a truly romantic night and want to keep it private. You know your guest list better than anyone. If yours is a "party all night" crowd, New Year's Eve could be a fantastic date for you.

VALENTINE'S DAY

When thinking of the most romantic day of the year, the first day that comes to mind for most people is Valentine's Day. The biggest pro for having a wedding on Valentine's Day is that it is not a popular time of the year to get married in most major cities, and therefore you will have more options for your wedding. The second pro is that couples love to dance, eat, and drink on Valentine's Day. What better way to celebrate than a wedding?

In terms of possible cons, because Valentine's Day is centered around couples, once again you may find guests who simply want to keep Valentine's Day private. Valentine's Day is not always on a weekend, either, so it may be more difficult for everyone to free up the day (and possibly surrounding days) for your wedding.

Setting the Tone Early On

While some couples who are planning their own micro wedding (and paying for it themselves) don't feel the need to communicate their reasons for having a smaller wedding with their families, others (such as couples with families who intend to help pay for wedding expenses) will want to set expectations for the sake of budgeting and/or family politics.

Micro weddings tend to be super personalized, and couples almost always manage their own planning process. If your vision for your wedding does not coincide with your family's vision, and they are funding much (if not all) of the day, difficult decisions and compromises will most likely have to be made. Be prepared to manage expectations when it comes to budgeting and picking the date (to allow certain family members to attend).

Managing Expectations

When starting to plan, you will need to manage not only your own expectations but also those of the people closest to you. While any wedding requires careful management of the guest list, the fact that your micro wedding will have just fifty guests or fewer means either your families will need to drastically reduce the number of people they invite, or you will.

And when it comes to managing expectations in terms of money, there may be a harsh reality to accept. If you and your fiancé are set on having a micro wedding and you don't have the funds for what you want, you will most likely need help from your family. If your parents are not happy about a smaller wedding where they don't get to invite all the people they want, be prepared for a conversation or to readjust your expectations to what you can afford without help. Once the tone and expectations are set, you will be ready to move on to budgeting.

Budgeting a Micro Wedding

The *B* word—*budget*—seems to strike fear in the hearts of many, but it can actually be a helpful guide and a tool for managing resources. You can leave your financial worries behind in order to enjoy your engagement by creating a realistic budget!

Money Matters

Money is normally the first item on the agenda after announcing the engagement to family. Be prepared for a very long list of questions from anyone who will be contributing financially to your micro wedding. If you plan on paying for the event yourself, you will have more control over your wedding day. If you are not having a traditional Western wedding (where the parents of the bride pay for almost everything), then you are either completely in control or will encounter more people to manage. Keep in mind that you have two families coming together. Sometimes money is no object for a family. For others, money can be a source of stress and tension. Tread lightly!

Tighter Budget? No Problem!

The majority of couples don't have unlimited budgets. If money is especially tight, it's best to prioritize those things that are most important to you for your wedding. Your job is to construct a budget based on your desires, using the resources you have available. No matter your budget, there are creative ways to make sure you can include all of the important elements of your dream day. Check out the DIY ideas in Chapter 10.

Who Will Pay for What?

Once you know what your overall budget is and what things you really want for your wedding, you'll need to figure out exactly how you're going to afford it. Who will pay for what? This question is very important at the beginning stages of the planning process.

> **fact**
>
> If you are holding a multicultural wedding, you must consult with each set of parents to understand each other's culture. In some cultures, the groom's family pays for everything. In Western culture the bride's family pays for a majority of the items. Be prepared to be flexible and listen.

You must have a face-to-face conversation (or phone conversation) with everyone who is paying for part of the wedding. Communication is essential.

Tracking Your Expenses

After setting your budget, determining how things will be paid for, and doing all the research into vendors, you can insert the cost ranges for each element of the wedding into your budget. The best way to keep costs organized and ensure they fit within your budget is to set up a spreadsheet. You can find a cost spreadsheet in the Appendix to either fill out or use as a guide to create your own version.

The only way you will be able to figure out an approximate cost of the goods and services you want for your wedding is to ask for proposals. Request bids from two or three wedding professionals for each category of service or good you are looking for. This will give you more negotiating power and will help you to see the average costs of each type of wedding professional. Insert these averages into your budget spreadsheet.

Consider a Wedding Planner

For a long time, wedding planners were seen as a luxury. However, as weddings have gotten more elaborate in recent years, more and more couples are opting to hire a professional coordinator to help them stay organized and as stress-free as possible.

> **essential**
>
> For many couples, etiquette plays a role in the wedding planning process. Some socially acceptable rules of manners or behavior are written, and others are not. Whether you care to follow any of these rules or not, a wedding planner will be your best source of advice on proper etiquette.

Most wedding planners offer four packages:

1. **Day of Coordination.** This is the most basic package that a wedding planner or coordinator will offer. Day of Coordination packages usually include:

- Help with your timeline.
- Logistical planning and help the month prior to the wedding.

- A walk-through at your ceremony and reception location(s), often done with the sales representative from your caterer/restaurant.
- Managing your rehearsal (if you have one).
- Coordination of your vendors with a head consultant (and an assistant, if necessary) the day of the wedding.

2. **Partial Consulting.** This level of planning includes everything in a Day of Coordination package in addition to help with the following (keep in mind that every wedding planner is different and may offer variations of these items):

- Help with crafting your budget.
- Recommendations of vendors that will be able to work within your timeline, budget, and style.
- Additional logistical management or help with important meetings with vendors (e.g., food tastings and conversations with photographers).

3. **Full Consulting.** In addition to services offered in both the Day of Coordination and Partial Consulting packages, Full Consulting is like having a personal concierge and advice service for every aspect of your wedding. The planner will be available for finding vendors (and subsequently go to any meetings needed with them), negotiating on your behalf, and helping with various levels of advice in terms of your wedding planning process. Most wedding planners will help with the overall design of your wedding day as well.

4. **Destination Wedding Consulting.** A destination wedding consultant will provide anything from the Day of Coordination to Full Consulting packages. However, because you are planning a wedding in a different city than where you live,

you will probably need to pay the travel expenses for this planner. It is highly recommended that you contract a destination wedding planner who lives in your area. This way the planner is available to meet in person when needed. Some destination wedding planners will be specialists in certain types of destinations (like Europe, the Caribbean, or Africa, for example). However, most experienced destination wedding planners will be able to pull off a wedding anywhere in the world because of their acumen when it comes to being able to handle international logistics well.

> **fact**
>
> Most destination wedding planners are experts in micro weddings, as most destination weddings are micro weddings. These consultants are well worth their fees in helping you find the right vendors anywhere in the world within your micro wedding budget and style.

Hiring a wedding planner is a welcome relief to many couples and can help bring back the excitement of being engaged! Should you decide to hire a wedding consultant, keep several things in mind. The first thing you should know is that an independent wedding consultant is your representative in the wedding industry. Do not confuse an independent wedding consultant with a wedding consultant who is part of a store, reception site, or caterer. These consultants cannot advise you on wedding professionals outside their area of expertise, or on products or services that they are not providing.

No matter who you hire for your wedding day, it is important to ask questions. Here is a list of key questions that you should be asking before hiring your wedding planner:

- How long have you been in business?
- Can you provide a list of references?
- How many staff members do you have?
- How many weddings do you handle per weekend/day?
- What are your fees? (Are they hourly? A flat fee? A percentage?)
- What is included in your package?
- Will you be the person coordinating the day of? If not, when can I meet my planner?
- Do you have photos of any recent weddings you have planned?

Professionals will be expecting these questions and will be happy to provide any requested information and materials. Many planners won't charge a fee for an initial consultation.

Is This My Wedding?

Whether you ask a wedding planner or a friend to help you with planning your micro wedding, be sure you are in charge of the decision-making process. In the end, it is your wedding day! Although it is not typical for wedding planners to make contracts with wedding professionals on your behalf, some planners do, as they take a percentage of sales from each vendor. If your planner has the power of the checkbook (or credit card), be sure you have a written agreement that you have final approval over who is being booked for your wedding day.

essential

You can ask your wedding planner to distribute gratuity envelopes to vendors for you on the day of your wedding. It is also a nice idea to include a well-written thank-you note with your gratuity to each vendor so they can show it to future clients.

If you are having difficulty in selecting your wedding planner, references are a great help! The best references for a wedding planner are, of course, couples who have used their services. Another great resource for finding a planner are venue managers, as they often work with wedding planners (if it is a popular venue). Some venues even print brochures with a list of recommended planners among other event professionals. If your planner is one of the best in the area, venue managers will know. Parents of couples who have used a particular planner are also a great barometer of how a planner will treat your family during the planning process and the day of the wedding. The best consultants have a wide range of styles and budgets in their repertoire. In terms of money, a general rule of thumb is that you should never spend more than 10 percent of your overall budget on a wedding planner.

Chapter Three

The Guest List

If there was ever a decisive moment in planning any wedding, it is when a couple creates their guest list. The special part about having a micro wedding is that it puts the focus on who you really want to have at the wedding. There is little room for obligatory invites. Formulating your bridal party also plays a role in the final guest list, and the venue will help set the tone for your invitations. In this chapter, you will determine who absolutely needs a seat at your ceremony—and who doesn't.

Set a Maximum Number

As you've learned, the maximum number of guests at micro weddings is typically fifty. A micro wedding is meant to include your families, your wedding party, and your closest friends. Most micro weddings end up being between ten and thirty-five guests total, especially when the engaged couple has small families and/or no wedding party.

A wedding with ten guests or fewer feels more like an elopement. If you are dead set on keeping your guest list at ten or fewer, and your parents are not in agreement with this maximum, it's wise to plan for the possibility of adding guests to your list if your venue has the capacity for more. You can also seek out a venue that has a set maximum close to the number you and your partner want. The right venue can help shape the day (and guest list) you envision.

---

alert

Be prepared for pushback from various family members if you want a small wedding and you have a large family. Your wedding day does not get a repeat, so setting up parameters from the beginning will help avoid difficult conversations later.

To help determine your maximum number of guests, start out with a list of everyone you would like to invite. It may turn out that a small ideal number is easily within your reach. Regardless, set boundaries for your list and stick to them. In most cases, the guest list is divided evenly between the two families, regardless of who is paying for what. Couples often split the list three ways: each set of parents and the couple; each set invites one-third of the guests. However, many couples, especially those paying for their wedding, believe they should have full control of the list and invite who they want. No matter the route you decide to take, keep in mind you have two families coming together. Working with the desires of your families can make the difference in how smoothly your union begins.

Don't forget to include your attendants and their plus-ones, as well as your officiant and their spouse in the final guest count. Everyone should also receive a formal invitation even though most are likely well aware that they are invited. See more information on invitations later in this chapter.

Children on (or Off) the Guest List

You may decide that you want a child-free wedding. In this case, you will want to be sure that your parents and the wedding party are aware of your decision early on.

Whatever you decide regarding children at your wedding (or any guest parameters, for that matter), everyone needs to stick to the same rule. You can't make an exception for your favorite cousin, who happens to be under your determined age limit. If you do, it is a sure bet that other parents will ask, "What are they doing here if my child couldn't come?" The only exception to this rule is if you're inviting your own children, or if children are participating in the ceremony. For example, if you want your nephew to be the ringbearer or your daughter to be the flower girl at the ceremony, it is perfectly reasonable to have them at the reception.

> **fact**
>
> If you end up having a small number of children in your ceremony (like a nephew or your own child), try to provide a babysitter or nanny service for your adult-only reception. Parents of these children will be grateful!

Depending on the size of your families, choosing a child-free wedding could make narrowing down your guest list much easier. Or you may decide that including the young members of your families will help make the day special and you can fit them into the smaller guest list without too much finessing.

Who to Invite (and Who Not to Invite)

So now that you have a maximum number of guests you are willing to have and you know whether or not you want to include children, it's time for one of the biggest parts of your wedding planning process: deciding who gets to be on your wedding guest list! Of course, many couples focus on immediate family first. Then you will need to consider other relatives, coworkers, and, of course, friends. Whatever you decide, choose early and decisively.

Coworkers and Distant Relatives

Your coworkers and distant relatives will most likely be the first set of people to be scratched off your list. Most micro weddings have nothing to do with the politics of where you work, and some distant relatives probably do not even know you on social media and have no idea you are engaged. If you need to cut the guest list and you feel comfortable excluding work acquaintances, this may be the way to go. If your distant relatives ask, tell them you would love to have them, but since you are having a small wedding, you are not able to invite everyone.

Friends

One of the biggest decisions you will make when inviting guests is deciding which of your friends can be invited to your micro wedding. Family will typically come first. However, some friends feel like family. Whether it is a lifelong friend or close friends from college, you will want to ask yourself, "Will these people be a part of my life ten, twenty, thirty, or even forty years from now?" Your guest list is small and you want the people who will support you and your marriage through its ups and downs to be there. The friends you can turn to for real advice. With a small guest list, tough decisions need to be made but these decisions could end up making strong friendships even stronger.

Miscellaneous Guests and Last-Minute Invites

You will probably allow any guest in a serious relationship to bring their significant other. It is also nice, but not necessary, to allow unattached guests to bring someone if there is space on the guest list. This is especially thoughtful for people who may not know many others at the wedding; it will help them feel more comfortable during the festivities.

Married guests should always be invited with their spouses. Always give your attendants the option to bring a date as well, even if they are not involved with anyone when you send out invitations. Your attendants spend a fair amount of money to be part of your wedding. Allow them to share the day with someone special to them.

You may decide to have a "B" list of guests to be invited if a number of "A" list guests decline to attend. Wedding invitations usually go out six to eight weeks before your wedding day, so your "B" list guests won't be offended if they get an invitation earlier or one that is close to the six-week cutoff date. (More on "B" and "C" lists later.)

Divorced Family Members

If the divorce between your parents was amicable, you won't have anything to worry about. If, however, the relationship between former spouses is at best unpredictable, you will need to map out a plan to deal with family tensions. The best way to prevent problems before the wedding is to speak with the divorced set of parents or relatives openly and honestly. All you can reasonably do is request their cooperation and ask them to be on their best behavior.

The majority of parents will try to put aside their grievances for this one special day, but it is always best to take precautions. Remind parents and relatives how important this day is to you. To be on the safe side, don't require divorced relatives to interact with each other. Seat them in different places at the ceremony and at the reception. Be sure they are surrounded by their own family and friends.

Out-of-Town Relatives

When inviting out-of-town guests, be sure you keep in mind the expenses that are involved for both them and your family. If a grandparent, cousin, or other relative is coming in from out of town, some family member may feel obligated to house them. If so, it is imperative that you offer financial help if it is needed to offset the costs for hosting that relative. They may not accept the offer, but they will forever appreciate it!

"B" and "C" Lists

Where your focus is on keeping your guest list small, you should always keep a "B" or "C" guest list handy for those who you would really like to invite in the event that you get any "regrets" RSVPs from your first round of invitations. This is easy to do without hurting anyone's feelings by sending your first round of invitations earlier than usual or even asking them to RSVP to your Save the Dates (or on your wedding website). The likelihood is that there will be some guests who will be unable to attend due to various reasons. Make sure you and your partner have agreed on the "B" and "C" guest lists ahead of time.

The Wedding Party

Your wedding party should consist of the most important people in your life, and you have the right to have as many or as few attendants as you want. Most couples having a micro wedding end up with a smaller wedding party due to the small number of guests in general. However, when creating your wedding day, you make the rules.

Family As the Wedding Party

Your family members can absolutely be part of your wedding party. If you don't want to leave your many siblings out of your wedding party, include all of them! One member of your family can also be your officiant. Many states allow people to be officiants for a day, or many become certified online.

Some states also offer couples the ability to self-officiate. (Check with your state or local government authorities to find out all about officiating in your area.)

Virtual Attendees

With micro weddings on the rise, more and more couples are opting for virtual online services to help include others on their wedding day. Whether your reasons for having a micro wedding are due to budget, privacy, or health concerns, online streaming options give couples the ability to expand their guest list! Like any product or service, there are different levels of streaming services at different price points.

Social Media Attendance

While several platforms are available for video conferencing at weddings, the simplest and cheapest is having friends and family connect to others through their cell phones. Some couples set up joint *Instagram* and *Facebook* accounts to instantly stream their weddings on a smartphone or other device. While the video quality is not necessarily stellar, it gets the job done! People can see you get married and you can record the streaming as well.

DIY Virtual Conference Platforms

There are many virtual videoconferencing software tools available for any type of event, including Zoom, GoToMeeting, Google Meet, and Webex. Keep in mind, this isn't just any meeting: This is your wedding. When it comes to videoconferencing online, be sure you understand how the platform works or enlist a friend to help you. The biggest challenge for online streaming tools is choosing the best location to set up the computer or video camera. In many cases it's easiest to have a videographer move the camera to focus on any important parts of the ceremony.

> **fact**
>
> When weighing your options for taking care of virtual guests, be sure you know exactly what your budget is and what you want. Online streaming tools are less expensive than having a professional livestreaming service as a vendor, but the quality is less predictable.

Some couples only want the ceremony to be streamed while others want to film the entire day. Be sure you know exactly what you want, and take an honest look at the pros and cons of having a friend or relative handle this part of your day.

Professional Online Streaming

Videographers and DJs should be the first two wedding professionals that you ask about online streaming. They tend to be more tech savvy than other vendors and have the capacity to take care of online streaming for your remote guests. Many DJs have to use online elements with their equipment and music anyway and are comfortable with the technology. Videographers are a natural choice, especially if you had already planned on using a videographer for your wedding day. While these professionals might not have all the same bells and whistles that some audiovisual (A/V) companies do, they will most likely have the best price, especially if they are already doing the music or videography for the day of the wedding.

When it comes to streaming your micro wedding ceremony for virtual guests, you need to weigh the pros and cons of doing it yourself versus paying a local company to perform this service. The main issue here is your budget. In almost all cases, having a professional provide streaming service will make for a seamless experience. Professionals are trained in streaming and have various types of plans to help design a customized experience for your wedding. Every wedding is different and will require different solutions.

---

alert

Livestreaming can be fraught with technical issues. While it might seem easy enough to DIY this, you may want to think twice if someone special (like your grandmother) is at the other end of the streaming. This is your wedding day, so take the time to find the right person or company to minimize any problems.

Many A/V and tech companies offer specific online conferencing packages and will likely be the best bet in terms of quality as well as recording capabilities. During the pandemic of 2020, a new crop of local online streaming companies sprang up all over the world in order to accommodate the burgeoning need for online meetings. Since then, these companies have continued to enhance their services and options available for all types of events, including weddings. Ask for references just to make sure the company you are interested in knows all the ins and outs of weddings, online recording, and live feeds. Streaming a wedding is very different from streaming corporate events, and most general A/V companies don't focus their marketing on weddings.

Many times, companies providing streaming service will forget to turn on sound or will be connected to an unstable Wi-Fi or cell phone network feed. Be sure the technical support you are getting from a professional is kept in check by at least one person attending your wedding. That person can monitor the feed and report any deficiencies in service.

Invitations

Your Save the Date cards and invitations should reflect the style of your wedding and venue. By the time you send your wedding invitations, the majority of your guests will probably already know the date, time, and place of your micro wedding. But even though we live in a wireless age, some people *need* something to stick on their refrigerator as a reminder. Whether you send your Save the Dates or invitations online or through the mail, it is the only way to keep track of who's coming and who's not coming, providing that people pay attention to your request for RSVPs.

Save the Dates

The Save the Date card is a relatively new and Western concept stemming from the information age. Save the Dates can be sent via regular mail, courier service (both domestically and internationally), or email. Some couples even record Save the Date videos that can be viewed online. The Save the Date can be particularly helpful for couples who have a lot of out-of-town guests who will need to start planning for travel and transportation early on. If you decide to mail a Save the Date, here are some example layouts:

Save the Date Example 1:

Save the Date
Robin & Michael
are getting hitched!
06.17.2023
Washington, DC
Invitation to follow

Save the Date Example 2:

We're Tying the Knot on the Beach!
Kelly + Roberto
6.10.2023
Cabarete, Dominican Republic
Invitation to follow

Save the Dates can be made into all sorts of keepsakes. You can include a photo or make it into a magnet, bookmark, or postcard. How about a fun photo-booth strip of the two of you holding signs that say "Please"—"Save"—"the"—"Date" (with the actual date on the last photo) in the four different shots? Then place a detachable magnet on the back so it can be placed on the refrigerator!

> **essential**
>
> Since Save the Dates are generally informal correspondence, it is best to keep the message as simple as possible. If you have a lot of out-of-town guests or it's a destination wedding, send a preliminary list of hotels that are near your ceremony and reception sites. Also, if you have created a wedding website, include that address as well.

Save the Dates will help you to get a clearer idea (much earlier than invitations) as to which of your guests on your "A" list are coming. Save the Date cards usually do not come with an RSVP card but almost always include your wedding website for additional information. You can have a section on your wedding website for RSVPs. If you learn early on that several of your "A" list invitees are unable to attend, you can pull names from your "B" list when the time comes to send invitations.

Where to Find the Perfect Invitation

You'll find several options available when choosing the style of your invitations. Whether you want traditional paper or online invitations, be sure you choose a style appropriate to the occasion. The most obvious place to shop is at a brick-and-mortar stationery store, but an even more popular place to find the perfect invitation is online.

Paper Invitations

A stationery store gives you the opportunity to evaluate the feel of the paper's weight, texture, and quality. If you are unwilling to order invitations online without that knowledge, request samples from the online store (most are willing to do this). Always ask to avoid buyer's remorse.

> **fact**
>
> If you normally have a hard time making decisions, take someone along who can help you narrow down the choices. Though the store employees will be of great assistance, your friends or family will be the voice of reason if you find yourself overwhelmed by all the choices.

If you are trying to have a less formal affair, be sure your invitations reflect that by using fun and informal wording. A whimsical look to your invitation will help showcase the informal vibe you are going for on your micro wedding day. Conversely, an elegantly engraved invitation is always appropriate for the most formal wedding.

Online Options

Just like the online Save the Date option, invitations can be sent online as well. Keep in mind that not everyone is connected to the online world. If you choose to do an online invitation, you may want to purchase a small number of printed invitations as well. You will need to mail an invitation to those who you know do not have email addresses (or who rarely check their email accounts). Most invitations come in minimum sets of ten or twenty-five, so order accordingly.

Printing Methods

The type of print you choose is a big factor in how much your wedding invitations will cost. There are a few printing options to choose from.

ENGRAVING AND LETTERPRESS

Engraving is the most elegant form of putting ink on paper. The printer creates metal plates and stamps the paper from the back, creating raised letters on the page. Stationers will tell you that this is the best form of printing to produce exquisite detail. You will end up paying extra for all that elegance, so unless you have a generous invitation budget, engraving may be off limits.

Printing of a similar quality is available with letterpress. This method uses firmly pressed inked letters from a polymer plate onto a single sheet of paper. The type sinks into the surface, creating a dense image on paper. This process is less expensive than engraving.

COST-SAVING PRINTING METHODS

A great way to get the look of engraving without the cost is through a process called thermography. Most mass-produced invitations these days are done using this method. By using a special press that heats the ink, the printer creates a raised-letter effect that is almost indistinguishable from engraving. What is distinguishable, however, is the price. It's about half the cost of engraving. Offset printing, also called lithography, produces flat images and is the starting point for thermography options.

Traditional Invitation Etiquette

Having trouble figuring out how to word your invitations? You're not alone. With all the mixed families in the world today, many couples find themselves wondering how to word invitations without offending anyone. Don't worry! There are as many styles of wording as there are styles of invitation. Note that in all cases you should spell everything out: names, the year, the time, and so on. It's perfectly fine to abbreviate common titles (such as Mr. and Mrs., for example), and it's also fine to use the numerical representations for the address of your venues, but only if you must. Generally, the address (including the street name) of a house of worship can be omitted altogether, unless doing so may cause confusion. (If, for example, you're getting married in New York City, you would need to specify *which* Saint Andrew's you've chosen for your wedding site.) If your entire guest list knows your wedding area well, however, and it's in a smaller location, you can simply opt for the name of the ceremony site, followed by the town on the next line. Zip codes are never included.

The best thing to do if you are having difficulty wording your invitation is to consult with your stationer or wedding planner. If you are buying your invitations online and you don't have a wedding planner, there are thousands of examples of invitation wording online, and most stationery websites have helpful guides. Just be sure all sets of parents take a look before you make a purchase.

Divorced Hosts and Deceased Parents

Circumstances will vary when divorced parents host a wedding, and a deceased parent is usually not mentioned on wedding invitations because only the hosts of the event are listed. However, if you want to mention a late parent, it is your choice.

Military Ceremonies

In military weddings, rank determines the placement of names. If the person's rank is lower than sergeant, omit the rank, but list the branch of service. Junior officers' titles are placed below their names, followed by their branches of service. Titles are placed before names if the rank is higher than lieutenant, followed by their branches of service on the next line. Refer to the Appendix for examples of how to address invitations and envelopes to those with a military title.

Invitation Extras

As if choosing the invitations and carefully wording them weren't enough, you'll also have choices to make about the envelopes, and how you want to alert your guests to the particulars of your wedding weekend.

ENVELOPES

Like the invitations themselves, the envelopes you choose can range from simple (with plain to high-quality paper) to elaborate (with ornate paper and liners).

---

alert

Before you break the budget, keep in mind that the envelope is a throw-away item. Ask yourself if it really makes sense to spend extra on something most people toss in the recycling bin. Remember, you can ditch this altogether if you plan on sending online invitations.

Beautifully packaged invitations are a lovely touch, but of course, the more you add to the envelope, the more it will cost.

PREPRINTED RETURN ADDRESS

Plan to have the return address preprinted on the outer envelope and on the response cards. Traditionally the address will be for whoever is listed as the host for the wedding. If you are the one communicating with the reception site coordinator or caterer (even if your parents are the actual hosts), you may prefer to have the responses sent directly to you. That way, you don't have to bother your parents every week (or every day, as the wedding gets closer) to see who has responded. Before you decide to put yours as the return address, make sure you tell the wedding host, just so you don't step on any toes.

RECEPTION INSERTS

If the reception is at a different location from the ceremony, you have a couple of options. For formal invitations, you should include a reception card. For informal invitations, you can simply write out the reception site's name, city, and state at the bottom of the invitation (if there is room).

When you are including a reception card, be sure to write out the full address of the reception site. For your out-of-town guests, you may want to insert a directions card instead (explained later in this chapter), which will include the address of the reception.

RESPONSE CARDS

You will need to include response cards with your invitations. Each response card also needs an envelope unless you are providing a postcard as a response card. In either case, you will need to affix a postage stamp for your guests.

Try not to be too hard on those oblivious souls who neglect to respond. A simple phone call or personal email (one that tactfully passes over their failure to RSVP) to ask whether they will be attending is perfectly fine once the RSVP cutoff date has passed.

DIRECTION CARDS

It may be necessary for you to send a direction card with your invitation, particularly for your out-of-town guests. These cards should not be as large as the invitations and should be similar in size to the other inserts. It should include general directions to the ceremony and the reception. The direction card is also the best place to remind your guests which hotels you have blocked rooms for (or recommend). You can also put your wedding website address (if you have one) on an information or direction card insert.

If you decide to put your wedding website on your direction insert card, you should never mention anything about the registry! Simply state: "For more information, please see our website: [website URL]" at the bottom of the card.

Remember, none of your guests is required to give you a gift, so no invite inserts should provide information about gifts.

Addressing the Envelopes

Give yourself plenty of time to address your invitations and be realistic. Remember that this is supposed to be fun and exciting because you're sending out your wedding invitations! So make a night of it. You can use your own handwriting or consider a calligrapher for a classic and romantic touch.

alert

Never use a printed label to address a wedding invitation envelope. Stickers on envelopes looks as if you were too busy to take the time to personally invite your guests, and they look like junk mail in a mailbox. Don't run the risk of your guests throwing your invitation away. You may *feel* that busy, but don't let your guests know it.

Don't forget to take a fully assembled invitation to your post office to weigh it to determine the exact amount of postage needed before you start putting those "love" stamps on all of the envelopes. Then choose what type of stamps you want to use.

Make sure the same person who writes the information on the inside of an invitation also addresses its outer envelope. This makes the invitation package look uniform and conveys that it was put together with care. Also know how to address people of various professions. Examples are as follows:

- A judge is addressed as "The Honorable [First name] [Last name]."
- A member of the clergy is "The Reverend [First name] [Last name]."
- A lawyer is addressed as "[First name] [Last name], Esq."
- Medical doctors are addressed as "Dr. [First name] [Last name]" (but PhDs do not require any title).
- Everyone else is "Mr. [First name] [Last name]," "Mrs. [First name] [Last name]," or "Ms. [First name] [Last name]"; these are the only abbreviations (aside from "Jr.") that are acceptable.

Everything else (with the exception of street numbers) is written out on the envelopes. Of course, you can always employ a calligrapher to take care of all of this for you! Well-trained calligraphers know the ins and outs of traditional addressing etiquette and will almost always ask you questions when you send information to them that is outside of normal etiquette (as the previous information is not an exhaustive list!).

Formal versus Informal Invitations

When addressing the outer envelope, include the full name of the person or persons you are inviting. On the inner envelope, you can be more casual. If you're addressing the outer envelope to Mr. and Mrs. Stephen McGill, feel free to write "Steve and Linda" on the inner envelope, but only if they happen to be your close friends. Otherwise, drop the first name and simply address the inner envelope to Mr. and Mrs. McGill.

> **fact**
>
> There are some invitation companies that can print both inner and outer envelopes for you. Printing addresses is less formal and less personal than handwriting them, but perfectly acceptable (not to mention incredibly time-saving). Printing addresses is almost always less expensive than hiring a calligrapher.

If you are inviting the whole family, the approach is pretty much the same. (Children's names should come after their parents'.) Children who are over eighteen and are invited to the wedding should receive their own invitations, whether they're living at home or on their own.

One more note on those inner envelopes: Remember how careful you had to be when addressing members of various professions on the outer envelope? You're not off the hook yet. While you addressed the judge's outer envelope, "The Honorable [First name] [Last name]," on the inner envelope, they are simply "Judge [Last name]." "The Reverend [First name] [Last name]" is transformed into, simply, "Reverend [Last name]."

"And Guest"

When you invite a single person with a guest, you're faced with two schools of etiquette: old school and actual world. Old school etiquette soundly denounces the use of the phrase "and Guest" on the outer envelope of an invitation *or* on the inner one. In the actual world, however, invitations are addressed this way all the time—and everyone understands it.

Bottom line: If you want to toe the etiquette line, you'll address separate invitations—one to the guest you're inviting and one to *their* guest. This will require a considerable amount of effort, in that you'll have to track down your guest's guest's address at a time when you're incredibly busy (which is why most couples shun this practice). If you want to make things easier on yourself, address the outer envelope with the name of your friend or relative. Then add the phrase "and Guest" on the inner envelope following their name or write out the guest's name if you have it.

Additional Paper Items

Your business with printers and stationery suppliers may not end when you order the invitations. Depending on the type of wedding you are having (and where), you may need various cards for entrance to the ceremony, special seating, or weather-related contingencies. You'll need some thank-you notes, and you may want to print formal announcements. It's always nice to have the thank-you cards match your invitation suite, but they don't have to.

When to Order

Order your invitations at least three to four months before the wedding, and always order more than you need. Don't assume you won't make any mistakes while you're addressing all of those envelopes. As careful as you might be, it can still happen! The last thing you need is an argument with your partner because they messed up the last one. Ordering at least twenty extra envelopes will lessen the tensions among those writing them out and will save you the cost of having to place a second order. (The majority of charges for your invitation are for the initial start-up of the press; adding a few more to your initial order is much cheaper than ordering again.) Even if you don't make any mistakes, you'll probably want to have a few invitations as keepsakes (for you, your parents, etc.). When tallying up the number of invitations to order, don't forget to include all of the people who will be at the rehearsal. This includes attendants, siblings, parents, and the officiant, along with respective significant others. Although a reply is not expected or required, these people may like to have the invitation as a memento.

---

essential

Plan to mail out invitations about six to eight weeks prior to the wedding, with an RSVP date of two to four weeks before the wedding. This will allow you time to give the caterer a final head count.

Be sure to leave yourself plenty of time to address and stamp all those envelopes. If you're planning a wedding near a holiday, mail out your invitations a few weeks earlier than otherwise to give your guests some extra time to plan. If you plan to invite more guests on your "B" and "C" lists as regrets come in, send your invitations out at least eight weeks in advance, with a response date of at least three weeks before the wedding. Pressed for time? Ask if your printer can provide you with the envelopes in advance. That way, you can write them out while the invitations are being printed.

How to Handle Those Left Out

One of the most difficult things that couples deal with when it comes to their micro wedding is how to handle the people who are not invited. While you may have a ton of great friends and a larger family, when it comes to micro weddings, there will most likely be people who will not be invited.

In order to help people feel included, you can do fun things with those people outside of the wedding day. You can host a fun dinner, a game night—anything that you love to do as a group. Of course, livestreaming your wedding will help those people feel included as well. If you have the budget and the time, you can also send copies of your program and maybe a recipe for your signature cocktail with the ingredients included. The sky is really the limit here. During the pandemic of 2020, many couples sent care packages (see more about care packages in Chapter 8) or had their caterers send boxed meals to those who could not be at the wedding. In most cases, people will understand why they are not invited, and the additional expense of trying to help them feel included may not be necessary. You are the judge of who those people are.

Chapter Four

The Venue

Once you know your guest count, the next step is to find a place to have your reception. Some experts say you should find your ceremony space first, while others say you should find your reception venue first. Whichever camp you belong to, you want to find the right space that is interesting for both you and your guests. Some reception spaces will be the first to be booked simply due to their popularity. Also, many places have the capability of having both your ceremony and reception all in one location. This chapter will help you determine the reception space that is right for you.

Finding the Perfect Venue

Your venue sets the tone for your event. If you are looking for a swanky and modern feel to your wedding, be sure to look for new hotels going up in your area and interesting venues and public spaces. Smaller and interesting boutique hotels are usually the best bets for micro weddings. If you are looking for something out of the ordinary and exclusive, think about a destination wedding. There are so many ways to set the tone for your big day. Don't set your date in stone until you have found the perfect venue for your micro wedding.

Another very important topic to keep in mind is that the reception space is where the bulk of your decisions are made and where most of your budget is allocated. Finding the right reception space, which dictates the flow of the day, is what the party is all about!

> **alert**
>
> During peak wedding months (timing varies in every country, state, and city), competition for popular wedding reception spaces can be cutthroat. If you are marrying in a large city, plan on securing your venue at least one year in advance. However, people cancel or reschedule events all the time, so get on a waiting list if they have one!

Some couples like the convenience of having the ceremony and reception in one space. Others love having their ceremonies in their places of worship or outdoors in a special place that has meaning for them. Whichever choice you prefer, be sure to look for ceremony spaces that could be a "just in case" backup for your reception space as well.

Event Venues, Mansions, Hotels, and Restaurants

Event venues, mansions, hotels, and restaurants are usually the mainstay for weddings as most of these options have private dining spaces that have different size capacities. Event venues and mansions have interesting spaces or can break apart larger spaces with airwalls or room dividers to accommodate the smaller guest counts of micro weddings. Most towns have interesting buildings run by local governments, and there will likely be some private options that might be perfect for your micro wedding.

Mansions and hotels might sound like "big" venues, but many (especially smaller boutique hotels) have interesting personalities and smaller spaces that are great choices for micro weddings.

Restaurants are also a nice fit for couples looking for a particular type of cuisine at their wedding. When booking an event venue, mansion, hotel, or restaurant, there are several factors to consider.

Event Venues

Event venues (also called "function halls") cover a wide range of locations. In many buildings that are owned and operated by nonprofit organizations, private event spaces are available that organizations use to hold their own meetings. These locations will usually be the most economical. Since meetings in these locations tend to be held on weekdays, weekends are usually reserved for event rentals.

> **fact**
>
> In the United States (and some other countries too), a certain portion of the fee for renting nonprofit facilities can usually be deducted from your income taxes. Be sure to ask the organization if they have information on tax deductions.

To be clear, every city has its own event culture. The term *function hall* will be recognized but not widely used in most cities. Most wedding planners simply call function halls "event spaces" or "venues," because *function hall* is a very general and outdated term.

Mansions

Almost every city has mansions that are either run by local governments or owned by private organizations or families to rent out for events. While many couples planning a micro wedding will shy away from a mansion for their wedding (thinking that it is going to be too large or overwhelming for the number of guests that are coming), they happen to be some of the best spaces for micro weddings. Mansions normally have a few different rooms that are beautifully decorated and may include a theme. Some mansions also double as galleries or museums, creating a sophisticated backdrop for a wedding.

In most cities, mansions that are often booked for weddings have outdoor spaces and gardens that are perfect for al fresco ceremonies. And if an indoor ceremony is more your style, having just fifty guests or fewer makes it easier to have a magnificent wedding in a gorgeous smaller space inside the mansion. A mansion may not have a lot of indoor space to fit regular dining tables, but it may be a perfect place to have a tented outdoor reception.

---

fact

Search engines like *Google* and *Pinterest* may be helpful for gathering ideas for a venue such as a mansion, but many cities have new venues opening or have hidden gems that only experienced wedding planners will know about. Research if a wedding planner might work within your budget to help you in your search for the perfect venue.

Many mansions have added spaces that might have specific points of interest to fit your wedding style, like conservatories, libraries, greenhouses, outdoor mazes, fountains, gardens, and more. If you are looking for a particular type of room (like a library, for example), this is where a wedding planner will come in handy. The more specific you are about what you are looking for in a mansion, the easier it will be for your wedding planner.

Hotels

Hotels are some of the easiest places for couples to plan their micro weddings. Most hotels are set up not only for housing but also for entertaining your guests for a weekend wedding. Larger hotels in any city will usually have their own catering department as well.

Hotels tend to work best for couples who plan on having a lot of out-of-town guests, and many (if not all) hotels have standard wedding packages.

---

essential

While most hotels will offer package pricing, don't assume that a package will be the cheapest option. Some hotels are extremely popular and can get away with higher pricing for their packages. Consider the price difference between catering at an off-site venue space versus the in-house catering at a hotel.

The other great advantage of a larger hotel is that you can almost always have your ceremony on-site as well. Many religious officiants can come to a hotel to marry you in an outside garden or backup ballroom or small meeting space.

Restaurants

The number one reason that most couples opt for a micro wedding at a restaurant is the style of cuisine. Many caterers have an amazing way of being able to replicate all kinds of foods from different cultures. However, when it comes to weddings, some couples really want to have the restaurant where they fell in love as part of their wedding day.

Here are some other reasons for having your micro wedding at your favorite restaurant (or a restaurant you really like):

- You won't have to deal with rentals and setup costs, as the restaurant will have their own tables, chairs, linens, glassware, and plates.
- The restaurant has authentic cuisine that reflects a certain culture.
- Many couples love being at high-end and highly acclaimed restaurants for the experience of having multiple courses in a well-known space.
- The restaurant is located near the ceremony location.
- The restaurant has a gorgeous interior that matches the vibe of your micro wedding.

In the end, many micro wedding couples love restaurant venues as they feel welcoming and less formal. A micro wedding in an intimate setting like a restaurant can feel more like a night out with your favorite people as opposed to a stuffy, formal sit-down meal.

Vacation Rentals

Many websites and apps are dedicated to renting vacation homes both in areas that are local to you and those in destination cities for your wedding day. Vacation rentals are the most popular things going for micro weddings and elopements. Just be sure to consider a few vacation options before starting your search.

Large Mansions and Beach Houses

When renting a vacation home, always pay close attention to the details about what is and is not allowed on the property. Some larger mansion owners prohibit parties on their properties; their biggest concern is that you might trash the place. You may be able to message the owner on the app you are using to ask for an exception if your micro wedding is small enough. Some owners are perfectly happy to host your wedding but may require an additional fee for staffing and security purposes to ensure all facility needs are taken care of during your wedding. You will want to take advantage of extra staff. If the fee is reasonable, it will be worth it to have someone making sure toilet paper and cleaning supplies are available and helping with any maintenance issues. For example, maybe the florist needs access to the water hose to fill vases out near the tent instead of having to lug forty vases from the kitchen and get in the way of the caterer. All sorts of things can happen at a wedding, and venue managers can answer questions and provide solutions.

Lofts and Penthouse Spaces

These spaces are the most common for vacation home rentals in large metropolitan areas like New York City or Chicago. These spaces are modern urban oases and have high-end style that may match your wedding's aesthetic.

Destination Wedding Vacation Rentals

When it comes to destination rentals, look for large homes in other countries that have owners who are able to speak with you in your primary language. This way, if you have particular questions about the space, they will be able to understand and answer accordingly (and nothing will get lost in translation). The other thing to consider is that some eco-lodges (smaller boutique hotels on beaches) may be listed as vacation home rentals even though they are lodges or hotels. These venues are always a great option as they will be able to help with finding other vendors for you and will most likely be able to provide the catering you will need.

Public Spaces

If the term *public spaces* makes you nervous, fear not. Many public spaces have building and outdoor spaces that can be rented to remain private for your event. Here are a few examples.

Public Parks

Having your wedding at a public park has major advantages but also some disadvantages. While many parks have incredible locations, scenery, and gardens, no amount of flowers or gorgeous landscape will make up for the fact that your wedding is in a public place, which means anyone visiting the park could take photos of your wedding and invade your ceremony space and privacy. If it is a popular space like the Thomas Jefferson Memorial in DC or Central Park in New York City, be prepared for onlookers and possible chatter around your ceremony. However, some public parks and buildings can mark off spaces for privacy. Be sure to ask the event manager for information.

Gardens

Gardens have long been a wedding staple. Depending on your city and the time of year, there may be some interesting casual gardens or botanical gardens available for your wedding day.

---

essential

While falling in love with a garden at a venue is wonderful, make sure you love (or at least like) the backup space for your ceremony. Many couples forget about this issue and just assume rain couldn't possibly happen on their wedding day. Don't make that mistake!

Many private homes have incredible gardens—maybe they are one of your neighbors! When it comes to getting married, gardens are the holy grail of modern micro weddings.

Museums

Museums are some of the most popular places to hold a micro wedding. Since museums are very careful with how they conduct any event in their space, be sure to check the museum's website before going to look at spaces for your micro wedding.

---

fact

Museums can really show off your personality. Some are non-profit as well. Many museums are multifaceted and have multiple spaces with audiovisual possibilities. Ask about the amenities that they may offer to make your micro wedding easier, as well as the tax deductibility of their fees for renting the space.

Not every museum will host a wedding. Some have different fees for different days of the week, and some have specific time frames when you can actually hold your micro wedding. For example, a museum may be open to the public until 5:00 p.m. every day and can host your micro wedding later in the evening.

Museums that focus on architecture, archaeology, or nature are fun, interesting, and modern wedding locations. Many museums also have unique short-term exhibits that last for months at a time. You can even design your reception around the theme of an exhibit.

One thing that always seems to pique the interest of couples having a micro wedding at a museum is the fact that docents or tour guides are usually available for all of their events. This way your guests will get a chance to see all that the museum has to offer during your reception. The small number of guests you will have makes having these tours even easier!

The main question you should ask when considering a museum venue is: "Does this space fit our personality as a couple?" You may also be interested in a modern space or something rustic. Look around at all the large museums in your city, but don't forget the smaller, local museums that reflect your city's personality and history.

Galleries

Galleries are an absolute favorite for couples wanting a micro wedding. Art and culture enthusiasts love the idea of eating near a work of art painted by Frida or having cocktails with Picasso! There are also tons of retail-style galleries that sell artwork by living artists. Whichever gallery you go for, be sure you find out about all their rules and regulations. Protecting artwork is of the utmost importance to gallery owners and the event managers for their spaces. Also consider that, for the protection of the artwork, flash photography is usually forbidden.

> **essential**
>
> Be sure you know their availability before you get your heart set on that corner gallery! An art gallery's availability for weddings may be limited. Most small galleries are privately owned and will not have enough space for a ceremony, cocktail hour, and seated dining. Others are government-owned and may not allow weddings on the premises.

Another perk of some galleries is their access to artists. If you have the time to investigate all the artwork that is available at your favorite gallery, you may find interesting ways to incorporate it into your reception. Be sure to ask a docent or the events director of the spaces you are looking at about the possibilities of featuring a particular artist during your wedding (if the artist is still living, of course!).

In most metropolitan areas with larger museums, many of the featured artists are deceased or living but so famous that it might be astronomically expensive to have the artist present. However, that does not mean you can't have an artist at your wedding. Many larger cities also have tons of local artists that do live painting services at weddings. Contact a local entertainment agency that might have actors who can dress up like your favorite famous artist and possibly even paint!

Courthouses

The courthouse is the most commonly used space for small, intimate micro wedding ceremonies or elopements. Some micro wedding couples find that the courthouse option is the best way to go when it comes to eliminating another venue in addition to the reception space. This is especially the case if the reception space doesn't have the space for a ceremony.

While courthouses have been traditionally seen as elopement spaces, some couples are able to have a micro wedding with their entire family surrounding them, as many courthouses have enough space to hold thirty to fifty guests. Be sure to ask a representative from the courthouse about size and space before reserving it.

Backyard Weddings

For many couples, the perfect solution to a reception dilemma is having their wedding at someone's home. If you are lucky, you, your parents, or someone you know well will have a house and a backyard to accommodate your reception. What better way to celebrate the most important day of your life than in the house you grew up in or the backyard where you used to play?

> **alert**
>
> Don't assume that having a backyard wedding will make everything easier or save you a lot of money. A home reception can be *more* costly due to the amount of equipment that has to be rented along with cleaning, renovations, and landscaping.

Depending on the type of wedding you want, a home reception gives you a lot of flexibility. If you want a formal wedding in the backyard with a tent and a band, you can do that! If you want a good old-fashioned barbecue, you can do that too! Flexibility is the main draw for couples wanting to have their wedding at home. Of course, there are many things to consider.

Ceremony and Reception Spaces

Is your yard large enough for a ceremony and/or reception? Is your home large enough to accommodate all fifty guests or fewer inside for your micro wedding if you don't have a tent and it rains the day of (or if you want to have your ceremony and/or reception indoors)? Be sure to consult an online event space software website (like AllSeated.com or SocialTables.com) or your wedding planner or caterer to map out your space. You need space not only for tables but also for chairs at each place setting and room for waitstaff and your guests to walk in between tables.

Bathroom Considerations

Many large homes will be fine if your guests use the bathrooms within your home. This is an easy consideration if you are just having family or a smaller micro wedding. However, consider several things when it comes to bathrooms. Do you want your guests walking all over your house and going into the master bedroom to use the bathroom? Remember that people are curious and do curious things when alcohol is involved. Simply hiding your jewelry in the sock drawer will not be enough. Another issue is water capacity. Some homes simply do not have the capacity to handle fifty guests. Finally, if the idea of guests hanging out in your bathroom and looking in your medicine cabinet (because they will) makes you cringe, you will need to rent a bathroom trailer, which can be costly.

Alcohol

When alcohol is served at your home there are important things to consider. You can save a lot of money by buying your own alcohol versus having a caterer bring it for you. You can purchase alcohol ahead of time as well. Having your wedding at your home gives you some flexibility with your budget too. If you are on the tightest budget, who says you have to serve alcohol? If you have room for it, stick to just beer and wine. If you have a little more room in your budget, you can serve a premade cocktail just for cocktail hour. Obviously, if alcohol is the main feature at your micro wedding, go all out! Have a local brewery come in to do a tasting during your cocktail hour. Offer top-shelf liquors and a specialty bar, like various types of whiskey and scotches, or a fun margarita bar. The sky is the limit!

The other thing to think about is safety and liability when it comes to serving alcohol. Hire a caterer with a liquor license, or talk to your homeowner's insurance agent about purchasing a rider for the day (this is covered more extensively in the next section).

Wedding Insurance

It's always best to review your homeowner's insurance policy about liability issues when guests are on your property. Consider adding a rider to your insurance policy to cover any liabilities that may arise at the wedding. Another reason to have wedding insurance is to cover all your expenses should a natural disaster happen due to the weather (or if an unprecedented pandemic or other event happens), or if a vendor somehow does damage to your property when setting up or breaking down items. Talk to your insurance agent to find out all the options. The point of insurance is peace of mind and being able to cover your losses in case of extreme and unforeseen circumstances.

Landscaping

One of the biggest reasons couples end up scrapping the idea of a home wedding has to do with how their home looks on the outside. While the thought of hiring a landscaping company might scare you pricewise, it may actually be cheaper than renting a venue. One way to look at the cost of landscaping is to see it as an investment. Your home will have more curb appeal, and you'll enjoy the landscaping more in the long run by learning how to care for trees, shrubs, and flowers that you had planted for the wedding. With a little research, landscaping could end up being one of the fun things you plan that other couples don't get to do! And beautiful plantings will provide enduring, nostalgic memories of your wedding day for years to come.

Parking

If you have a large property, parking might not be a problem for you in terms of having fifty guests or fewer. However, if you only have a small driveway, you may want to consider hiring a valet service to ensure you don't annoy your neighbors. Valet services will manage the logistics of where to park cars without resorting to tearing up the landscaping you just spent money on. Your guests will appreciate being able to hand over their car instead of parking blocks away and walking to your house in their new high heels.

Tenting

"Should we get a tent or not?" is the question couples most frequently ask when planning their wedding at a private home. One reason you should at least put a deposit on a tent is that there is no way to guarantee the weather. If your wedding is a formal affair held in a backyard, a tent is a must if you have no indoor backup option.

Cleaning

Cleaning is the number one service that couples forget about when planning their wedding at home. No matter how careful you are to keep your guests outdoors—or close off parts of your home in the case of an indoor event—they will most likely come inside anyway. People are curious, and maybe the cousin you haven't seen in two years has not seen your new home yet. No matter the reason, consider hiring a cleaning service a couple of days prior to your wedding to help reduce stress and give you some extra time. Then, of course, a cleaning service after your wedding will be essential. You will most likely be exhausted and won't want to take out the mountain of trash and recycling that needs to go to the curb or your garage. Nor will you want to clean the bathrooms if your guests were using them all night long!

Destination Weddings

In most cases, a destination wedding is automatically a micro wedding. The average size of an international destination wedding is thirty-five to fifty guests. You'll find it's a lot easier to work with wedding planners or tour operators in other countries, but whoever does the planning, there are several things to consider when it comes to a destination wedding. The primary factors are location, travel logistics, and languages, which are detailed in the following sections.

Location

Obviously, the first topic to consider is which destination you want to have your micro wedding in. When choosing a location, you will want to look for smaller properties like boutique hotels, villas, eco-lodges, campsites, vacation house rentals, all-inclusive resorts, and golf courses.

With a small amount of people traveling, the possibilities are endless. However, here are some of the most popular destination wedding cities and countries from around the world:

- **Bahamas:** Known for its powder-white sandy beaches and turquoise waters, it is a great getaway for destination micro weddings. Its rich history, steeped in multicultural backgrounds, provides a mixture of English, African, and local customs, creating the perfect blend for a unique and beautiful wedding.
- **Bali:** Take your pick of interesting and provocative locations in Bali—the ocean, mountain, and lush tropical landscapes and interesting villas peppered throughout the country are perfect for weddings. It's also great for combining your destination micro wedding with your honeymoon. Bali appears

on many international lists as one of the most romantic and sexiest places on earth to honeymoon in.

- **Bermuda:** A smaller nation full of personality and pink, sandy beaches, this location makes the perfect backdrop for a destination micro wedding. With less than seventy thousand inhabitants and a historical British influence, locations range from a quaint, high-end bed-and-breakfast to a resort complete with world-renowned scuba diving and shopping (with plenty of gorgeous Vespas to go around)!

- **Dominican Republic:** Some call this country a paradise! It promises a wide variety of locations that are perfect for weddings—everything from beautiful beach and resort locations on the coasts to the fascinating city of Santo Domingo (the oldest city in the New World, where Diego Columbus lived). The Dominican Republic is also home to some of the world's most incredible mountain and river locations. With turquoise rivers, caves, and expansive protected forests along with plenty of country clubs (including Casa de Campo, which boasts one of the world's best golf courses), you simply can't find a more diverse Caribbean country. The country provides sustainable tourism options as well, with many eco-lodges and smaller boutique hotels to serve the eco-friendly couple!

- **Florida Keys, Florida:** The over 1,700 islands in the Florida Keys are divided into five main regions that together stretch about 115 miles: Key Largo, Islamorada, Marathon, Big Pine/Lower Keys, and Key West. These coral islands have great landscapes and are perfect for photos and couples flock to the Keys for the pristine water. Key West is best known for its snorkeling, scuba tours, kayaking, hiking, and exploring.

- **France:** While Paris may be the only city that pops to mind when thinking of a French destination wedding, there is no shortage of unique locations all over this romantic, art-loving country. Large estates, palaces, and castles peppered throughout the countryside remind you of the historical decadence and fashion-forward sense that this country has had for centuries. Other cities popular for micro weddings are Cannes, Bourges, Carcassonne, Versailles (you can get married at the palace, but be prepared for a long waiting list), Toulouse, Bordeaux, Lyon, and Nice.

- **Greece:** Here's a country perfect for island hopping, eating, and getting married! While Santorini is the most popular city for weddings, don't forget about Mykonos (popular among the rich and famous), Crete, Chios, Rhodes, and so many other islands. Known for white sandy beaches along the Mediterranean, Aegean, and Ionian Seas and its unmistakable cuisine, the Greek Islands have a rich history, with plenty of historic churches, chapels, resorts, and so much more to host your micro wedding.

- **Hawaii:** The state of Hawaii is made up of six major islands and has a wide variety of options for a destination micro wedding. Maui and Lanai tend to be the most romantic of the six, and Kauai is suitable for more adventurous souls. Oahu, Hawaii (the biggest island), and Molokai are less known for weddings, but these islands still have plenty of places for a micro wedding! Hawaii's rich historical significance and tropical island amenities offer no shortage of wedding locations. Keep in mind, though, that this state is located in the Pacific Ocean, and the best time of year that has the least amount of rainfall is June to September.

- **Italy:** Italy may be the number one choice for a European destination micro wedding. Almost every city in Italy has an incredible history that you have probably seen featured in movies and books! Rome, Florence, Milan, Venice, and the Amalfi Coast tend to be the cities of choice for most couples, as each offers something entirely different. Rome is best known for its rich historical and political significance with countless monuments and unique grand buildings (think the Colosseum, Pantheon, Trevi Fountain, etc.). Florence is known for its romantic and Renaissance arts backdrop and is also the capital of the Tuscany region. For those who love fashion, Milan will be the city of choice. Venice is known for its romantic and picturesque canals, shops, bridges, architecture, and history. And couples adore the wild-looking landscape of the Amalfi Coast, which looks like a colorful staircase of houses overlooking the sea.

- **Jamaica:** The food, culture, and incredible beach resorts with inexpensive packages make Jamaica the perfect place for a destination micro wedding on a budget (without looking like it)! The vibe is always laid-back, but the service at the major resorts is world renowned. Most Jamaican resorts are known for creating elaborate food displays for their daily guests as well as for weddings. It is one of the island's best kept secrets that Jamaica has some of the world's best chefs (there is so much more than jerk chicken and patties on the island).

- **Mexico:** One of the easiest countries to travel to from the US and Canada, Mexico is a popular micro wedding option for many couples. Its expansive beaches (like Tulum, Cancun, Maya Riviera, and Playa del Carmen) and attractions in Mexico City (think Frida) offer countless choices for location. Another fantastic element to Mexico is that it's easy to have your wedding in one location and your honeymoon in another, and usually it's inexpensive as well.

- **New York City:** One of the most famous cities in the world, New York City is one of the most interesting places to get married. The list of fabulous locations is endless, as long as you love an urban landscape or Central Park!

- **Portugal:** While Lisbon has long been recognized as one of the most beautiful cities in Europe with its gardens, trams, cobblestone streets, decorative ceramic tiles, and pastel-toned Gothic- and Renaissance-style homes, Portugal has so much more to offer. Cascais and Sintra are two main cities that are lovely for destination micro weddings. For smaller weddings, the cliffs at Praia da Ursa and Praia da Adraga are incredible, unique locations that are unparalleled by any other country in Europe.

- **Spain:** Spain has become wildly popular for destination micro weddings, as it has a key international airport hub in Barcelona, and its countryside and coast are easy to travel. Madrid, Valencia, Granada, Seville, and surprisingly, the sleepy beach town of Tarragona (with ancient Roman ruins to explore!) are great locations for micro weddings. Spain is friendly to tourists, and the number of abandoned ancient castles along with high-end gastronomy available throughout the country make it possible to have a micro wedding fit for a king or queen!

- **Thailand:** Chiang Mai, Bangkok, and Phuket are three of the most visited cities in Thailand, but they are only a portion of the absolutely breathtaking and epic countryside locations the country has to offer. In addition, you'll find some of the most exotic and delicious dining experiences on earth. One of the most impressive cities in Thailand is Sukhothai, which was once the capital of Thailand. This city and so many more are why Thailand appears in so many of the world's lists of best places to visit and get married.

- **United Kingdom:** The UK, which includes England, Scotland, Wales, and Northern Ireland, is an absolute favorite among destination wedding couples. With all the glorious landscapes, pageantry, castles, and the incredibly rich history throughout Britain, it's no wonder this country can be called the perfect place for a destination wedding. It's also important to note that most of the traditional customs for weddings in the United States stem from England as well.

- **Washington, DC:** Due to its diversity and international inhabitants from all over the world, Washington is considered a destination city. Many spaces in the Smithsonian museums are available for weddings (this was not allowed until 2019), and DC's historical monuments and architecture, multiple art galleries, and expansive estates make it an ideal wedding locale for history and politics buffs.

Travel Logistics

Destination micro weddings always add a hefty amount of travel logistics to your already full plate of wedding plans. If you have room in your budget, this is when a wedding planner, destination management/experience company, or travel agency will be an enormous help. The added stress of dealing with all of your guest's travel itineraries is enough to make most couples reconsider a destination wedding. These professionals will be able to help with not only the wedding logistics but also unadvertised excursions and experiences that are known only to the locals. You don't want to miss out on the hidden gems that might be available for you and your guests to enjoy.

However, if you are worried about the budget factor here, don't be. A wedding in the United States costs anywhere between 15 percent and 70 percent more than a wedding in most other countries. Most couples end up saving thousands of dollars when they decide to do a destination micro wedding. It's an option that's best for couples who are flexible and open to new ideas.

Language

If you decide to have your micro wedding in a country where you do not speak the native language, take heart: There are options! Most (if not all) countries listed in this chapter have tour guides in multiple languages (and English is one of the most spoken languages in the world, next to Mandarin Chinese). Tourism is an important source of income for those countries, so tourism guides and travel management agencies always have translators available for tourists and engaged couples alike. Anywhere tourists normally go and where people like to get married, tour guides and wedding planners can help with coordinating the wedding, travel, and everything else in between. You may also be able to count on a few of your guests to know the language of your destination. In other words, don't exclude any of these countries because of the language spoken there.

Plan for Rain

For any event that is going to be held outside, you will need to have a rain plan. Most venues have spaces that can serve as an indoor backup in case of rain. Others will most likely need tenting. Depending on your budget, be careful which venue you choose if you want an outdoor ceremony. Tents are a pretty hefty expense. Some venues have their own tents or special discounts with partnering tent companies, so be sure to ask about your venue's rain backup plans and any tent companies that work best with its facilities.

Chapter Five

The Ceremony

The greatest part of having a micro wedding is the ceremony. While the reception is always fun to plan, the ceremony is the real reason you are gathering your closest family and friends. Most ceremonies for micro weddings are very intimate and personal, as everyone in the audience is close to you and your families. With this intimacy in mind, there are several things to take into account when planning your ceremony. In this chapter, you'll explore the different kinds of ceremonies, whether to include family in your nuptials, and how to incorporate an online element.

Traditional or Personal?

You will need to decide whether you want a traditional ceremony, incorporating religious or cultural customs, or a more personal one with a mix of traditions and personal touches. Micro weddings are easier to personalize, especially considering the smaller number of guests you will have. Religious and secular wedding ceremonies alike have nuances that can make the content yours.

Nonreligious (Secular) Ceremonies

Some couples faced with potential family problems at interfaith ceremonies choose a civil or secular ceremony. Others go the secular route because they aren't particularly religious people, or simply to avoid the expense of a traditional church or temple wedding due to time constraints and/or budget. Civil ceremonies are usually quite a bit easier to plan than a traditional religious ceremony. But having a civil ceremony does not mean that you cannot have the ceremony of your dreams. An officiant can perform a civil ceremony anywhere.

Religious Ceremonies in Houses of Worship

The specifics of religious ceremonies vary widely from religion to religion and denomination to denomination. Your officiant will be able to explain in more detail what is involved. A religious ceremony does not necessarily have to be performed in a house of worship (such as a church, synagogue, or temple). It simply means that the ceremony will be performed in accordance with the laws or rules of your specific religious denomination. The most common religious ceremonies are Christian (Catholic or Protestant), Jewish, Muslim, and Hindu. The following sections explore the guidelines for each of these popular religions in more detail.

CHRISTIAN

It is important to understand that most Christian denominations have a base of similar beliefs taken from the Bible, but each denomination has different ways of performing religious wedding ceremony rites. For the sake of brevity, this section focuses on the most popular denominations in the United States, which are Catholic and Protestant denominations.

- **Catholic.** If you are getting married in the Roman Catholic Church, you will have extensive premarital requirements. First, there is Pre-Cana, which is the Roman Catholic Church's premarital course that every engaged couple must complete. Pre-Cana covers topics such as sex, finances, and children within the context of Catholicism. Once you have completed Pre-Cana, you will be given the option to have an entire Catholic mass, complete with the Liturgy of the Word and Eucharist, or a shorter version that includes readings, the priest's homily on marriage, prayers, exchange of rings, and vows.

---

alert

If you are a divorced Catholic, there are certain procedures that you will need to follow in order to be eligible for another ceremony within this denomination. You will have to go through a long annulment process (involving a church investigation and possible trial) to prove that your first marriage was not valid. Talk to your priest about the specifics and be prepared.

- **Protestant.** Protestant marriages, regardless of denomination, do not require premarital counseling. Normally a short informational meeting with the pastor of your church is required to gather information about you as a couple and to tell you about the customs of your denomination and the church where you will have your ceremony. The Protestant ceremony includes prayers, readings, exchange of vows and rings, celebration of Communion (normally for the couple only), the pastor's homily about marriage, and the benediction.

Ask your priest or pastor for additional information when planning your ceremony around a specific Christian denomination.

JEWISH

Judaism has different denominations with different rules. Jewish marriage in the Orthodox and Conservative branches have a few stipulations that require rigid adherence. Weddings cannot take place on the Sabbath or any time that is considered holy. Both Orthodox and Conservative ceremonies are recited in Hebrew or Aramaic only, and neither branch will conduct interfaith ceremonies. Grooms and all men must wear yarmulkes, and brides must wear wedding rings on their right hands. However, in most Jewish traditions, certain elements of the wedding ceremony are as follows:

- **The *bedeken* (veiling of the bride).** This tradition happens before the ceremony. The groom veils the bride.
- **Signing of the *ketubah* (Jewish marriage contract).** This marriage contract spells out the rights and responsibilities of the groom in relation to his bride. Ketubahs are usually gorgeous pieces of artwork that are displayed in the couple's home after the wedding. The bride, groom, rabbi, cantor, and sometimes witnesses will sign the ketubah.
- **The *kiddushin* (betrothal ceremony).** This part of the wedding takes place under a *chuppah*. A chuppah has four open sides and a cloth covering the top to represent a house of hospitality just like Abraham's tent from the Torah.

- **Seven Blessings (*Sheva Brachot*).** Here are the basics of each blessing, which the rabbi expands upon during the ceremony:

  1. The first blessing is about love in the context of marriage.
  2. The second blessing is about a loving home in the context of marriage.
  3. The third blessing is about humor and play within a marriage.
  4. The fourth blessing is about using wisdom in marriage.
  5. The fifth blessing is about health within a marriage.
  6. The sixth blessing is about art, beauty, and creativity within a marriage.
  7. The seventh blessing is about the community at large in relation to a marriage.

- **Blessed wine is taken from a Kiddush cup.** Most Jewish couples will want to have kosher wine, which is a wine produced according to Jewish law. Other couples who are not as religious will choose a white wine to minimize possible stains should the wine spill during the ceremony.
- **Groom smashes the wineglass.** This custom symbolizes the destruction of the temple in Jerusalem in A.D. 70. It is always followed by congratulatory shouts of "Mazel tov!" from the wedding guests.

- **Yichud.** Bride and groom retreat to a private room alone after the ceremony for about fifteen minutes to "consummate" the marriage. While many modern couples do not consummate their marriage on their wedding day, the Judaic law requires this fifteen minutes alone. Even if they do not consummate the marriage during this time, for many Jewish couples, it is a beautiful moment to be alone together right after the ceremony to take a breath and acknowledge that they are now formally and actually married! While some Jewish couples are not particularly religious, most love this tradition. Many non-Jewish couples have incorporated this practice into their ceremony as a beautiful tradition of reflection.

---

fact

You will most likely be hungry and thirsty from all the ceremony activities. If you decide to include the yichud practice into your ceremony, ask your caterer if they can provide you with some of the food that the guests will be enjoying during cocktail hour and maybe your preferred beverage.

It is always a wise idea to consult with your rabbi and extended family (on both sides) to determine what traditions and/or items can be worked into your ceremony to make it more special.

ISLAMIC

The only requirement of a Muslim marriage is the signing of a marriage contract. The *nikkah* is the ceremony where the bride and the groom sign the marriage contract. The contract includes the couples' consent to marry, the approval of the bride's guardian (called a *wali* or *wakeel*), the presence of two Muslim witnesses, and a *mahr* (the monetary value of what the groom will give to the bride). Depending on the Islamic sect you are associated with, all sorts of various cultural traditions and customs can be included in the actual ceremony. Some Islamic sects dictate a separation of genders throughout the ceremony and reception. Blessings are normally included in the ceremony, which are recited from the Quran. An imam or religious leader typically will oversee the ceremony, but according to some Quran and Islamic traditions, any trusted Muslim may officiate at the nikkah.

HINDU

There are many different traditional Hindu wedding practices as well as specifically Bengali wedding practices. You and your fiancé will need to consult with your families to make sure your ceremony reflects your families' traditions and heritage. Hindu weddings are based on three essential values: happiness, harmony, and growth. Ceremonies are normally performed by a Brahmin or Purohit (priest).

INTERFAITH CEREMONIES

If you and your fiancé come from two different faith backgrounds, your ceremony should include aspects from both your religions. The majority of interfaith ceremonies take place at the reception site. The most important aspect of an interfaith ceremony to consider is whether or not you will have officiants from both religions present. Consult your officiants to find out what is allowed within your religion.

Venues for Your Ceremony

Depending on your religion and culture, the ceremony location will vary. If you and your fiancé are of the same religion and want a religious ceremony, you may want to have your ceremony in your place of worship.

Ceremony Logistics

No matter your religion or cultural background, you will have some very basic decisions to make. Who sits where and who will walk with whom down the aisle are all very important concerns for you and your families. The following standards are based on traditional Western etiquette. Your decisions will be based on your own religious (or secular) and cultural traditions as a couple and what feels right for everyone.

SEATING OF THE GUESTS

If your ceremony does not include groomsmen, it is recommended to have at least one usher per fifty guests to help seat them. But many modern and nontraditional weddings do not include ushers at all. For traditional Christian weddings, the bride's family sits on the left side of the aisle (facing the altar) while the groom's family sits on the right side. The opposite is true for Reform or Conservative Jewish weddings. For Orthodox Jewish ceremonies, men and women are usually segregated.

Traditionally, your siblings and immediate family sit in the first and second rows beside or behind your parents (who are always in the front row). Grandparents and close relatives should never sit farther back than the third row. Of course, if your family is much larger, make the appropriate decisions on where family members should sit based on seating restrictions at the location of the ceremony. In some ceremonies, the first few rows of chairs are sectioned off by ribbons or signage to indicate that they are reserved for family. Most micro weddings do not adhere to this very specific set of etiquette rules, however.

PROCESSIONAL AND RECESSIONAL

Your processional can be as simple as you want it to be. Many micro wedding couples walk down the aisle individually or together. If you have attendants, make sure to have a rehearsal prior to the wedding to finalize the order of the processional. You can include your parents and grandparents as well in the processional, which is a more traditional approach.

In the recessional, the couple leaves the ceremony first, followed by any attendants, and then the parents and grandparents out of respect. After the parents and grandparents, it is up to you and your families as to how you want the rest of the guests to recess. Typically the rows closest to where the ceremony took place leave next and those farthest away leave last.

LGBTQIA+ Wedding Ceremonies

The legality of LGBTQIA+ (lesbian, gay, bisexual, transgender, questioning/queer, intersex, agender/asexual/ally, and also pansexual and the other countless ways that people self-identify) ceremonies will differ from country to country, depending on local laws. The legality of LGBTQIA+ weddings is mostly focused on same-sex weddings. If your country recognizes same-sex marriage, your wedding can be as simple or as elaborate as you want it to be, and it will also be legal. If your country does not, your rights as a legally married couple are hindered, but this should not prevent you from having the ceremony of your dreams. Your ceremony should reflect you and your families' heritage and beliefs, of course. Some religions do not allow for same-sex marriages, so be sure to consult your religious leader and family on how to personalize your ceremony and include your religious beliefs.

Religious and Secular Inclusivity

In many cases, LGBTQIA+ ceremonies cannot be held in a place of worship but can still include religious aspects. Even if an LGBTQIA+ couple's religion refuses to accept them as they are, it does not mean they can't incorporate their beliefs in a personal way within a secular ceremony. Many micro weddings are not held in places of worship for this very reason—to be able to include everyone (and their religious or secular beliefs) and to be free from having to conform to society-dictated "norms." To include their religious beliefs in a secular setting, couples may add religious text to be read during the ceremony, or incorporate symbols from their religion into the venue.

Educate and Illuminate

One of the most important elements in many LGBTQIA+ weddings is to educate others about the LGBTQIA+ community. *Educating* here does not come in the form of handing out pamphlets or reading from a book, but rather by adding a little more information than usual to the printed programs and in what the officiant says during the ceremony. You can also provide information to some of your guests prior to the wedding. When it comes to micro weddings, many guests may not need an education in what LGBTQIA+ means. Due to the small number of guests and your close relationships with them, everyone there will likely be aware. However, you will know better than anyone who needs to be educated in a friendly way.

The Officiant

Today, the number of interfaith and multicultural weddings continues to increase. Choosing your officiant may be as easy as calling your childhood pastor or as complicated as hiring two officiants from two different religions.

> **fact**
>
> The officiant of a civil ceremony is a judge or other official legally able to perform a marriage. Where will you find your officiant? Contact your local city hall or courthouse in person or online to find specific information for your city. Each officiant will have their own fees unless you get married at the courthouse.

If you are not religious, secular officiants are always available for a fee, and officiants are also available at courthouses to marry you.

Your Religious Officiant

For some, hiring an officiant involves nothing more than calling their childhood pastor and setting a date. For others, this may be extremely complicated if you now live in a different city and/or your family is scattered all over the world.

Marriage is a very specific religious rite and therefore should be handled with care. Consult your families to be sure to find the best religious officiant for you and your fiancé's religious ceremony.

Interfaith Officiants

If you and your fiancé are from two different faith backgrounds, you may want to consider a nondenominational officiant. If having officiants from both religions is complicated or unacceptable to one of the religions, the easiest solution is to have your ceremony at your reception site and hire an officiant who can incorporate elements from both religions. However, if both religions allow officiants from both religions to be part of the ceremony, divide the responsibility between the two of you to find the appropriate officiant for each of your religions. Both officiants will normally meet ahead of time and discuss what they think is most important for your ceremony to best reflect your two families coming together in a loving way (and to make sure it flows well). Typically, both officiants will stand together throughout the ceremony and will take turns performing various elements that are required of each religion (and what you both want during the ceremony). Keep in mind that this will make for a longer ceremony, but it will be appreciated by family members attending the ceremony.

Including Family and Friends

There are so many ways to include family and friends on your wedding day! Later in this chapter, you will learn more about how to include guests who will be attending virtually. Here, you will learn how to include the guests who will actually be present at the ceremony and reception.

> **alert**
>
> Many micro wedding couples opt to have more guests present at the ceremony only and have a reduced guest list at the reception. It is the one way to have all guests present for at least part of the micro wedding. You can have a separate invitation for just the ceremony, then have a separate invitation insert for the reception for the smaller micro wedding guest count. You can also consider having all the guests who attend the ceremony be part of a simple refreshment reception at the same location, and then have a more intimate and elaborate dinner reception later for a smaller guest count.

Your wedding will consist of the people you love the most and the people who are closest to you in your daily life. Having them included on the wedding day is of utmost importance in creating a special, personal experience. While this list is certainly not definitive, here are some easy ways you can make sure that everyone feels included and part of the day:

- Have one of your guests help with addressing and sending off your invitations.
- Have a few of your guests deliver care packages for the wedding day to your guests who will be local and virtual only. (See Chapter 8 for more information on care packages.) Be

sure their task gives them enough time to get back home and get ready for the wedding. The logistics of this may get tricky if a large number of guests need these care packages. If the care package does not include perishable items, you can also deliver them a day or two before the wedding with instructions. If you are mailing the care packages, have your friends or family help you package the items and make the trip to the post office for you.

- If someone you know has expertise in graphic design, ask them to help you design your invitation and even a wedding logo.
- Have a group of invited friends help you come up with the best hashtag for your day for social media purposes.
- Enlist a friend who knows calligraphy (or has beautiful handwriting) to help address your invitations or write out your escort or place cards.
- Have someone help with doing your makeup or hair the day of the wedding.
- Have someone help you with the development of your favors if you are providing any.
- If one or more of your guests are great at baking, ask if they can make a few special desserts for the wedding that you know everyone will love. It can also be a huge money saver to have a dessert bar instead of a wedding cake. Be sure to thank each person who baked for you with a handwritten thank-you note to be dropped in the mail the day of the wedding or left at their place setting.

essential

It is important to note that some venues who provide catering will not allow outside food from other vendors. Often a wedding cake is allowed, but if you're planning individual desserts, be sure to ask before you are disappointed the day of the wedding.

- Consider asking a family member or friend if you can use their home for a welcome reception if you are having out-of-town guests.
- Have your parents or a friend host a brunch at their home the day after the wedding.

In the end, you know your family and friends and their talents! Utilize what they do best if you want to include them (and they are willing to help). You can also ask them if they have any ideas for ways they can contribute to the wedding.

Chapter Six

Wedding Style

Wedding style is broken into two categories: what you will be wearing, and the actual style of your overall wedding day design (along with a possible theme you may be creating). This chapter will help you consider the various caveats of what you will wear along with how to go about creating the design of your micro wedding. Creating a mood board or gathering photos of what makes you happy will be the best place to start when it comes to the overall design of your overall wedding. It is helpful to have your board ready as you begin reading this chapter. If you don't know how to make a mood board, you can always enlist the help of a wedding planner. Other places to get help are online resources such as *Pinterest* and *YouTube*, and wedding websites such as *Wedding Wire*, *Style Me Pretty*, *Wedding Chicks*, and *Ruffled*.

What to Wear

"What will you wear?" is usually one of the first questions you will be asked after you have announced your engagement. And it has been that way for centuries! When Queen Victoria of Great Britain married Prince Albert of Saxe-Coburg and Gotha in 1840, she did so in a white gown (when it was not a popular color choice). She literally changed the history of wedding gowns, as almost all wedding gowns leading up to that point were in all sorts of colors!

For most of the last two centuries, wedding dresses have been mostly white or ivory. However, once we crossed into the twenty-first century, couples started to buck the notion that brides should only wear white, and grooms should only wear tuxes (or very formal suits like morning suits or military formalwear). In the United States today, it is rare that a groom would even think of wearing a morning suit (or morning tails) at their wedding—let alone even know what a morning suit is!

The greatest thing about having a micro wedding is that you get to wear what you want that day. In fact, you can have fun including nearly everyone who will come to your wedding in your chosen style of clothing.

question

Why did Queen Victoria go against tradition for her gown?
Queen Victoria donned her white gown for the love of her country. Her hope was that by wearing a white gown made with lace, she could help the failing industry of lace designers in England! It was a remarkable thing to do as a queen in a time when dresses were seen as a way to represent status and wealth (especially in political circles).

Want to have an outdoor glamping-style micro wedding at a local winery or in your backyard? Surely you won't want everyone dressed to "the nines." And what if you love the color blue and are having only ten guests? Consider having everyone wear something blue and make that your nod to the tradition of "something blue"! Your personal style and imagination (and possibly your religion and culture) are the only limits to what you can do at your micro wedding. Your venue may also help guide the theme of your clothing choices, making decisions that much easier. The following sections will help you brainstorm ideas and make judgments for what the two of you, your parents, and your guests will wear the day of your wedding.

Brides

At a micro wedding, it is all about wearing what *you* want to wear. If you want to go super traditional and wear your mother's gown or a new couture gown, you absolutely should! If you love how you look in black and feel your best in that, wear a black dress! There are no rules except for being true to yourself and your partner. Remember, Queen Victoria wore white when no one else did, so why can't you be a queen and wear red, pink, or green on your wedding day?

Of course, you may need to factor a few things into your decision. If both of you are brides to be, for example, you will have to decide what each of you wants to wear. And if two cultures or religions are coming together, you will need to consider your attire a little more carefully as well. Check out the next sections for more information on these facets of wedding fashion.

TWO BRIDES

When both of you are brides, the options are truly endless. If you want to go the route of a wedding dress, you can either both wear wedding dresses, or choose to have one of you wear a wedding dress. If one or both of you want to wear suits, the choice is also up to you. You can wear different colors and express each of your individual styles through your wedding outfits.

DIFFERENT RELIGIONS OR CULTURES

A wedding is one of the most important rites of passage in almost every religion, and many require specific elements to be included. An important thing to keep in mind is where you are getting married. If you are having a formal wedding in your place of worship, plan accordingly and respect its customs. You may be bending some of the wedding "rules" of society at large, but that does not give you permission to be rude or disrespectful in a place of worship (or anywhere, really).

---

alert

Remember, you are marrying into another family and their culture. You don't want to begin the marriage with cultural and religious conflict. Your wedding day is one day; your marriage is for a lifetime. Carefully planning a multicultural wedding is a whole other book indeed!

If you are adamant about what you want to wear (and it doesn't fit the protocols of the place of worship), you will need to hold your ceremony in a secular location. If your fiancé practices a different religion from your family, you will need to communicate the wedding clothing options to the ceremony officiant(s). If your officiant is strict, you will need to consider having two distinctive ceremonies (so as not to offend). Many couples decide to have two ceremonies for various reasons. Be respectful and always ask your families' and your officiant's guidance on the matter so that you can honor each side of the aisle.

Grooms

Micro weddings are all about individual style, and this definitely applies to grooms! Men have had little say in the past about their wedding day attire. A formal affair demanded grooms wear a tux, morning tails, or military formalwear. Up until the twenty-first century, most men assumed that the bride was the center of attention on the wedding day, and they were just an accessory. Micro weddings have changed this for the better. These days, men make more decisions about what will happen on their wedding day. The most important change for grooms has been their mark on the style of their wedding day. After the start of the twenty-first century, the wedding industry saw more men wearing khaki pants or less formal suits at their weddings instead of tuxedos. While plenty of grooms still wear tuxes or morning tails, this is usually the groom's choice. Micro weddings have taken it a step further. When you have fifty guests or fewer, the *couple* becomes the center of attention. Smaller weddings tend to focus much more on what the couple likes as opposed to the guests' experience. This is not to say that guests don't have a great time at smaller weddings; it just means that smaller weddings mean more room in the budget to reflect the style of the couple. This includes the groom's tastes. Men are becoming more and more involved in every aspect of micro weddings.

> **fact**
>
> When the COVID-19 pandemic hit the wedding industry, almost every wedding became a micro wedding because of the limitations on the number of guests allowed. Grooms became more involved in the planning as they saw how heavily their fiancées and their families were affected by the pandemic and how much money was lost to previous plans for a big wedding.

Grooms now have more choices in literally all aspects of the wedding, including what they are going to wear. Of course, grooms should have always been important because it's their wedding day too!

Grooms, like brides, have to balance their fashion ideas with a few caveats. See the bride's section earlier in this chapter for notes on how to handle a wedding involving two different religions or cultures. But what if there isn't a bride at all?

TWO GROOMS

The main thing to keep in mind with a wedding for two grooms is that you get to do you. Two grooms don't necessarily have to wear two different suits, nor do you both have to wear suits at all. If you and/or your partner want to wear a dress, wear a dress. If you want to have two entirely different suits, you should definitely do that. If you want to be "matchy-matchy" because that suits your style as a couple, then by all means, get matching outfits! This day is all about the expression of your love and your style combined.

Parents

Parents have it easy—they almost always choose what they will wear on their children's wedding day. Mothers try to find an outfit that makes them feel comfortable and beautiful, and fathers usually follow along with whatever the couple desires for the men's outfits that day. Micro weddings are no different in this aspect.

---

essential

The best advice for directing your parents' style choices for your wedding is not to direct them at all! Make suggestions and leave it at that. Most parents want to make their children happy on their wedding day and will take the suggestions. If not, don't sweat it, and keep the wedding planning moving forward.

Talk to your parents about their preferences. Consider letting them express their own style as it will make for a better relationship with your in-laws after the wedding is over with. Micro weddings help you to focus on what matters the most. Your parents are the wedding guests most likely to be involved in your lives as a married couple after your wedding day. You can let your parents know about the color palette so they might dress in accordance with it. However, they may want to wear different colors. Their style choices are usually what makes them feel most comfortable and confident. Determine whether a palette or individual self-expression is more important to you, and communicate your thoughts.

Guests

The style of what guests will wear at any type of wedding is something very difficult to direct. Most engaged couples do not make a lot of direct suggestions, and it is usually not necessary as many of your guests may simply ask you.

> **alert**
>
> Keep the guest fashion requests light. Be careful not to be too overbearing about it. In the end, you are having a micro wedding because you want it to be a meaningful day. Every guest list is different, so act accordingly and go with the flow.

Etiquette suggests you make it known when you are having a black-tie affair, especially if the venue requires it (an exclusive club, for example). However, with micro weddings, you can have a little more fun if you are having a less formal wedding and have easy communication with all of the guests.

> **question**
>
> **How do we communicate to guests about our wedding style?**
> The best suggestion is to pay for it. Since most micro weddings are small, you might have more wiggle room in your budget to purchase something for them. Consider sending your guests scarves or ties (or something similar) in the mail along with your invitation to go along with your specific theme.

It is not hard to get in touch with fifty guests via email or a phone call to let them know you want them all to wear blue, if possible (for example), to be part of a fun theme. Some guests may dislike the idea of wearing your theme color, though, so be relaxed about the request if you are asking guests to wear something that they might not own or feel uncomfortable with.

Children

For most weddings, children are the easiest to "dress up." Younger children and newborns will be dressed by their parents, and you can always ask if parents would be willing to dress their children according to the wedding's theme. Most parents will love the idea. However, only you and your fiancé know how comfortable you think your guests will be in dressing their children up to be part of your style choices.

---

essential

Children are innocent in the "politics" surrounding the emotions of your wedding, and some children can be obstinate. If your ring bearer refuses to wear the cute bow tie you bought for him or the flower girl refuses to wear a dress, it's best to let them walk down the aisle in what they want to wear!

The rules for dictating what children wear to weddings are the same as they are for adult guests. You might have more say in what children will wear if they are in the actual wedding party or, of course, if the children are your own. However, as mentioned previously, each child is different and you will want to take a cue from the parents of the child.

Traditional or Personal Style?

The overall theme, style, or design of your wedding day is all about your *Pinterest* page or the mood board that you, your wedding planner, florist, or designer came up with for your ceremony and reception venue(s).

Traditional Style

Traditional wedding style will vary according to the culture of the area you grew up in and also where you will be having the wedding. This style also has a lot to do with etiquette and wedding rules and customs that date back centuries. A traditional micro wedding will include the traditions that many weddings adhere to, just on a smaller and more meaningful level. Many traditional micro weddings have the ceremony in a place of worship, followed by a traditional (or culturally acceptable) reception. Typically, traditional micro weddings will not have a ton of personalization beyond a chosen color palette. Traditional weddings, in essence, are more geared toward the couple's religion or cultural heritage as opposed to customization.

Personal Style

Personal style is about how you want to convey your personalities as a couple through the details of your wedding. You'll want to create an atmosphere that reflects the two of you. How do you do that? Lots of creative ways! One way that many wedding planners and designers try to find out your personal style is by looking at your wedding *Pinterest* page or mood board to understand the vibe you are going for. Other designers will start by looking at your personal decorating style in your home. A designer might look at how you like to travel (or not travel) along with your favorite colors. Colors you love tend to repeat themselves in your home, travel, and personal wardrobe. Also, think about what makes the two of you happy as a couple on a daily basis. Your wedding will reflect the two of you if the colors, food, and activities of your daily life are woven into the design elements.

Attendant Style

Attendant style has to do with how you incorporate your wedding party into your wedding and is not solely based on what they will wear (as was discussed previously in this chapter). Many micro wedding couples have fewer people in their wedding party, and some have just as many as a larger wedding might have. Keeping in mind that you will have fewer than fifty guests, the number of attendants will dictate the number of guests you can actually have at your wedding and your attendant budget. The more attendants you have, the more money you will spend on gifts, flowers, hair, and makeup for them—and the fewer guests you may be able to invite. Remember, it is customary to allow each attendant to bring their significant other. Choose wisely! Your attendants will play a major role in your micro wedding day as you will not have a large guest list.

Bridesmaids

Micro weddings have liberated women all over the world from the dreaded one-use, unattractive bridesmaid dress. Most bridesmaids know that swatches, a mood board PDF, or *Pinterest* link is coming with your color palette. You will be the best bride/groom ever by telling them to wear what they feel most comfortable in (within your color palette). When women wear what they want to wear and feel beautiful, the photos with your bridesmaids tend to be more natural, fun, and beautiful as well!

Groomsmen

Most micro wedding grooms tell their groomsmen to wear a particular color suit just as brides tell their bridesmaids to dress within a particular color palette. For example, if you want your groomsmen to wear navy, forget about designer details and let them wear their favorite navy blue suit. If everyone wears navy blue and looks and feels their best, that should be the most important thing. If you opt for a more formal style, you may let groomsmen pull out their own tuxedo from their own wedding, or let them choose their own style of tuxedo from a rental company. The choice is yours, of course. It may be easier and more cost-effective to rent all the tuxedos from the same company. Make the style of your wedding work for those who will be involved that day.

Flowers and Other Décor

Flowers and other types of décor play a huge role in creating a certain feel. Many couples opt for a smaller and more inti-mate micro wedding because they want a focus on their style and really love planning the décor of the event. A lot of your flowers and décor will depend on your venue and your color palette, so choose your venue wisely. It will dictate the style of your event. For example, if you go with a barn or rustic style reception venue, you will want to have more of an eco, boho, rustic, or shabby-chic style for your décor to complement that setting rather than clash with it. If you are having your wedding in an urban modern venue, you will want to go with more of an artsy, art deco, modern, or monochromatic urban chic feel for your décor. The following are some of the most typical floral and décor aspects for weddings and how you can brand them with your style.

Bridal Bouquet

The bridal bouquet is the most important floral design of the day. For the remainder of your lives together, a photo of the two of you will sit on your mantel, in your hallway, or on your bedside table. It may also be in your parents' home, your bestie's home, your siblings' homes—you get the idea. Most likely you will be holding your bouquet in that photo. Make sure that bouquet includes the flowers of your dreams! You can even have a bouquet that is completely different from the rest of your décor—it just needs to be something you really love.

---

fact

Bridal bouquets have been seen as a tradition passed down from one generation to another ever since photos have been available. Some brides bring photos of their mom's or grandmother's bouquets to florists to have them recreated for their wedding day, especially if done in remembrance of someone who has passed away.

If you don't really like flowers, use something you *do* like. If you love paper flowers, brooches, lanterns, wood, fruits/vegetables, ribbons, garlands, geometric shapes, or fans, this element can be worked into a beautiful "bouquet." Just be sure you make it as timeless as possible. Trendy accessories for weddings will quickly look dated.

Bridesmaids

Usually, the bridesmaid bouquets all match and incorporate your color palette. But you don't want these bouquets to compete with yours. At micro weddings, many couples choose flowers that the bridesmaids actually like. If you have three bridesmaids, for example, why not ask each of them what their favorite flowers are? The florist can then create bouquets using flowers that each bridesmaid loves, while matching them to your theme and color palette. This type of floral detail will make the wedding day more meaningful for your bridesmaids as well.

Mothers and Grandmothers

Find out what flowers your mothers and grandmothers love before you meet with your florist. Your florist can use favorite blooms to make a corsage or a pretty nosegay (small bouquet) that they can keep and dry after the wedding as a memento of the day. Lavender and roses are popular choices for mothers and grandmothers alike. If you decide on corsages, be sure to ask women if they want a wrist or a pin-on corsage. This will depend on the type of material and style of the dress or suit that they wear. If their outfit has delicate accessories or fabric, suggest a wrist corsage so the material isn't damaged by pins.

Flower Girls

This is definitely a floral design element that you can have a lot of fun with. Some of the more popular choices for flower girls are smaller bridal bouquets to match yours (so she feels super special), flower girl baskets with petals (traditional), hair crowns/wreaths, and kissing balls/pomanders. Keep in mind that most children that are two years old or younger often want to put flowers in their mouths. It is best to let very young children just dress up and look cute. You can always have a younger flower girl hold the hand of an older flower girl or have her parent walk or carry her down the aisle, depending on the child's confidence, maturity, and personality.

Groom

There are a lot of different things you can do for a groom. Flowers can match the bridal bouquet, or design something different for each groom if there are two. Be sure to ask your florist to cover the stem part of the boutonnieres in a ribbon, twine, or decorative wire that either matches the lapel of the suit jacket or the style of your wedding. The groom can also wear something nonfloral. If either of you are into microbrewing, how about some hops? One of you loves to golf; why not a tee attached to the lapel? If the groom plays the guitar, go with an interesting twist on a guitar pick. Alternately, a simple pocket square adornment keeps things simple.

Groomsmen

Groomsmen's flowers can match the bridesmaids', or you can design something unique to match the groom's vision. Or each groomsman can wear something that reflects their personality. The groom can work with the groomsmen to come up with something everyone is looking forward to showing off on the big day. Pocket squares work nicely for groomsmen too!

Fathers and Grandfathers

The best bet for choosing flowers for these important men in your life is to make sure the boutonnieres match their lapels (and match those of their partners or spouses). This way when the photographer takes their portrait, their flowers will be coordinated.

Siblings

If your siblings are not in the wedding party, you may want to provide them with flowers or another element that matches the theme, the bride's bouquet, or the groom's boutonniere. Be sure to ask them first if they want one. Not everyone likes to wear boutonnieres or corsages.

Welcome Décor

Welcome décor adorns the entrance to the place of worship or the reception site. If there is a foyer, consider placing a floral design or some interesting décor that matches that of the venue. If the venue is a hotel, that will be difficult (but not impossible). If you are the only wedding booked for the weekend at that hotel, ask the sales rep if their florist could provide florals that week that match the color of your event. You will never know unless you ask.

If you are looking for welcome décor for your outdoor wedding in a garden, field, or park, consider a pretty beverage station with a mix of spa waters, lemonades, and/or teas. Not only is a beverage station functional, but the displays can be beautiful, eye-catching, and match your wedding colors. If the color palette is pink and green, for example, why not have cucumber-infused water with pink lemonade? Is your wedding in the morning? Have a coffee or cappuccino/latte station with a barista. Having a brunch wedding? Provide a colorful mimosa station with fruits to match the colors of your wedding. Always look for ways to infuse color and your personal style. You can also opt for gorgeous entrance flowers or interesting décor to match your theme. If you have an eco theme, add some interesting artwork from a local artist, or rent some beautiful plants in different sizes with gorgeous pots or locally made boho chic baskets to hold them in. This décor can also be combined with various other items, such as:

- Programs
- Engagement photos
- Photos of previous generations and their weddings
- *Kippot* (yarmulkes) for Jewish ceremonies
- Warm blankets (if your ceremony is outside and it is going to be slightly chilly)

There are any number of ways to incorporate décor into your welcome displays.

Ceremony Décor

Your ceremony décor will vary depending on the venue, religion, and style. If you are having the ceremony at a place of worship, discuss options with your officiant. This could consist of various types of florals, candles, structures, and other possible décor for just outside the entrance of the building. If the ceremony is at a hotel, mansion, farm, barn, or park (or any other secular location), you will most likely have more options. You can choose to have a customized backdrop or free-form structure, arch, or trellis along with flowers and all sorts of various floral, lighting, and décor options. Here are a few popular, highly decorative, and meaningful setups for various types of cultural and religious ceremonies:

- **Mandap for Hindu or Jain (Indian) ceremonies.** This structure is usually very colorful. It has four sides and uses a fabric topper and sometimes side fabric draping. Many of these structures are hung with beautiful garlands of flowers. For almost all mandap ceremonies, there will be six chairs (two for the couple and four for both sets of parents). The two chairs for the couple are along the back side of the mandap so they are the focus for the guests. Each set of parents will be on the side of the mandap closest to their child. There usually is a decorative pillow for the officiant. Along with the structure are other elements that go underneath the mandap. There is almost always a fire element under a mandap, and floral garlands are exchanged. Depending on your family's traditions, there may be spices, fruits, rose petals, rice, and sindoor.
- **Sofreh Agdh designs for Persian ceremonies.** These layouts are beautifully designed with all sorts of elements for different aspects of the ceremony. A table laid with a piece of white decorative fabric and chairs for the couple are essential. Other

elements include a mirror, flowers, candelabra, holy book(s), rock candy, noghl (candied almonds), rose water, yogurt, fruits, honey, bread/cheese/green herbs, bread with *Mobarak Baad* written on it (which means "Congratulations" in Farsi), nuts, seven spices, seven colors of Espand (wild rue seeds that are tinted for the ceremony and burned to ward off bad vibes or energy), gold coins, a needle with seven colors of thread, sheer fabric (to hold above the couple during the ceremony), sweets, eggs, and sugar cones (Kaleh Ghand). Be sure to understand the very specific meaning attached to all of these items individually as they will be part of your ceremony. You may also include other elements from your family's own traditions.

- **Chuppah for Jewish ceremonies.** This structure is usually six feet square, and tall enough to house everyone who will be standing underneath it. The couple, the rabbi, and both sets of parents traditionally stand underneath the chuppah. You can also have pole bearers if the structure is not freestanding. The structure must be open on all four sides to represent how Abraham's tent was open for hospitality.

- **Decorative chairs and tables with gorgeous floral displays for Afghan ceremonies.** Emerald green is a color widely used for Afghan ceremonies. Whether it is what the bride is wearing or a nikkah shawl, the materials used are beautifully decorated and become family heirlooms. Emerald represents prosperity and paradise.

- **A tea ceremony for Chinese weddings.** In this tradition, the couple serves tea to their parents and other important family members. This represents the union of the two families and is done in each of the couple's respective family homes (traditionally the groom's family is served first). Most couples do this ceremony before a traditional Western ceremony (if they are having more than one ceremony), and it is almost always done on the same day as the wedding. You will need:

- A tea set (red is an auspicious color to use)
- Hot water
- Tea leaves
- Two chairs and a table
- Two pillows

Be sure to ask your officiant and family about all that is needed for a certain religious or cultural setup ahead of time.

Cocktail Décor

The cocktail hour is where you might place your escort card display, multiple small tables, plants, interesting lawn or indoor games, bars, and possible lounge furniture vignettes to match your style. In the next section, you will learn more about the comprehensive and customized escort card displays and signage available. Florals and simple décor elements for these smaller tables will depend on your personal style. Arrangements can be as simple as photos, candles, interesting seashells (for a beach wedding), framed trivia about the two of you, and almost anything that represents your theme. If you are highlighting a specific theme, here is where you can add certain smaller elements to show off your style.

Reception Décor

The reception is where micro wedding couples can really show off their personal style. Fewer guests means less money toward food and more money toward décor. This is one of the main reasons why couples decide to have a micro wedding.

If you have always wanted to have a vignette of antique furniture in the garden, do that. With a smaller guest count, you can get those expensive linens you have been dying to rent. Order those tall and lush floral centerpieces for your three tables! Get the hanging floral designs and specialty lighting décor for your customized dance floor. If you are a foodie, have a celebrity chef cater and maybe do a cooking demo during your dinner! The ideas for reception décor are unlimited and only bound by your style and imagination—another reason to hire a wedding planner.

Food As Décor

Food can be a wonderful element of your day. And if your food and beverage contract (discussed in more detail in Chapter 7) is close to half of your wedding budget, it should be considered a major part of your décor. Make sure your beverages, hors d'oeuvres, salads, main entrée, and desserts pop with your color scheme.

A few fun examples to get your creative juices flowing are:

- **Pretzels:** If you love pretzels, why not have a pretzel station with all the typical toppings and different types of soft pretzels available? Have your caterer or event designer come up with an interesting display for this to really show off your personality or have beer and pretzel tastings provided by your favorite local brewer.
- **Sushi:** Are you a big sushi fan? Bring in a sushi chef during your cocktail hour to whip up a few of your favorite sushi rolls and to make some special rolls on-site while your guests watch!
- **Cocktails:** Do you love tropical libations? Have a fun beverage station complete with a bartender who makes fun and

fruity island drinks. Your drink list can match the colors of your wedding and you can offer nonalcoholic options as well. Your caterer or event designer can get creative and make a fun display or bar for this (they might already have a fun tiki- or island-style bar available).

Dessert As Décor

Don't forget that dessert is always an inviting tablescape that you can fully decorate (or hang from a tree or a ceiling treatment). Your wedding cake can be as over the top and decorative as you want it to be. But you can make your dessert budget stretch farther by having a beautiful or adorable cutting cake in addition to a table full of amazing different desserts that the two of you love (designed in your color scheme, if you like).

> **essential**
>
> Many micro wedding couples make the mistake of offering only a fabulous cake and don't recognize that many people suffer from allergies or food sensitivities. Pay attention to the dietary restrictions of your guests! Colorful Parisian-style macarons, meringues, certain types of chocolate candies, and flourless chocolate cakes are popular gluten-free wedding dessert options.

Even people who don't like sweets appreciate the beauty of a dessert table. You can add interesting linens, a few different and colorful cake stands (or three-tiered stands), flowers, and unique pieces of décor.

To help gather your thoughts and prepare to meet with your florist for décor and fashion elements of your micro wedding, see the Floral Design Worksheet in the Appendix of this book.

Signage

Signage is usually the last thing that couples think of when it comes to wedding style. But it's the *first* thing that guests see when they are welcomed to a ceremony or wedding reception and the last thing they see as they leave. For micro weddings, signage can really kick your décor up a notch. The following are some of the more popular ways that you can use signage as a major part of your micro wedding style.

Welcome and Ceremony Signage

One of the simplest and most cost-effective ways to take your micro wedding style to the next level is welcome signage. Maybe you are getting married in a large building and people need directions to your ceremony. Any guest who is unfamiliar with your venue(s) will appreciate directional signage. If you are having your ceremony and reception at the same venue, welcome signage will guide guests to the ceremony location first so that they don't end up in the reception spot too early, while vendors are still setting up finishing touches. Go for a look that matches the style of your venue with a pop of color or florals to help make it stand out. Welcome signage can come in a lot of different forms. Here are a few ideas to spark your imagination:

- Welcoming beverage station or decorative wall with your favorite alcoholic and nonalcoholic drinks (or simply interesting and colorful sodas, teas, or juices).
- A gorgeous wall, chalkboard, or table of information about how the day will flow.
- A display of your journey as a couple—showcase how your love unfolded as you show your guests where to go. A fun twist is to pose trivia questions based on the information.

Add the questions to each place setting and invite guests to compete for a prize.

If you focus on having fun and showcasing your personality and style, the welcome signage or display can be a lot of fun and gorgeous at the same time!

Escort Card Displays

Think about an interesting escort card display instead of the typical escort cards with a floral design in the middle. An escort card is the card that you pick up following the ceremony that tells you where you will be seated during the reception. A unique escort card display with interesting "cards" attached can double as an amazing backdrop for photos and social media. Don't just think in terms of actual cards for this. The majority of customized escort card displays double as favor displays. For example, if you're featuring a travel theme with luggage tags as favors, why not customize them for each guest at your micro wedding? Insert a gorgeously calligraphed table number inside each tag, then hang them on cute little color-coordinated hooks on your escort card display board. Have a signature cocktail or mocktail? Set up a cart outside the ceremony area with a fun treat or drink. Add an interesting accent with each individual's name and table number. Here are a few other fun concepts:

- Customized ice cream cup or vintage ice cream holder with a bamboo spoon featuring guests' names and table numbers.
- Fun milkshake with a straw that has a cute little paper flag noting name and table number (maybe find out ahead of time what each guest's favorite milkshake flavor is).
- Colorful cotton candy in a paper cone calligraphed with their name and table number.

Think of your favorite things that coordinate with your theme and color palette, and you can probably imagine what would be the cutest display ever! If not, contact a wedding planner or designer or check out ideas online for more inspiration.

Bar Signage

If you are having local and interesting beers, whiskeys, sodas, or a signature cocktail, consider having a nice sign made for the bar. Otherwise, the restaurant, hotel, or caterer will just print something simple to let your guests know what is available. Why not spend the extra time to make a cute or beautiful sign that you can frame and keep in your kitchen after the wedding as a reminder of your gorgeous day? If you don't know where to start, ask your invitation designer or wedding planner/designer for some help so it matches your theme or your invitation suite.

Reception and Dessert Signs

No matter what type of reception you are having, you will most likely have food! From the cocktail hour to the desserts (depending on your setup), you will most likely need signage for your food displays. Many micro weddings are all about the details, and food plays a big part in that. If you are having delicious hors d'oeuvres that have interesting ingredients (or ingredients that can affect people with dietary restrictions and allergies), labeling them with small tent cards or interesting menu displays will be important. Buffets need signs for each food item, and if you are having a family-style dinner, you will need printed menus or table signs indicating what is to come. Dessert displays need signs to let people know what they are eating as well. Get creative here and enlist the help of your stationer, wedding planner, or floral designer.

Chapter Seven

Food, Beverages, and Music

Food and beverage (F&B) contracts and music typically account for 55 percent to 60 percent of a wedding budget. However, one of the great things about a micro wedding is that F&B contracts are less expensive as there are fewer guests! It's important to work out the details of your F&B contracts first and then work through what you will be spending on the rest of your vendors such as music. In this chapter, you'll consider each of these three main elements of entertainment for your wedding day, from menu and catering logistics to the pros and cons of DJs versus live bands.

Your Menu and Catering

Although you and your fiancé may be too excited to eat much on your wedding day, your guests will be looking forward to the menu! Your goal is to find the right caterer to provide the cuisine to fit your budget, style, and taste.

Catering a micro wedding can be basic or complex. It might involve two people in a kitchen making tea sandwiches and hors d'oeuvres for an at-home reception or a full-service caterer supplying cuisine, tables, chairs, linens, dinnerware, and a full bar. Along with your budget, the type of reception you want will help determine the kind of caterer you need. Another form of catering is "in-house" catering at event venues that have their own kitchen, rentals, and staffing (like hotels). The following sections explore the nuances of catering and how to approach it as an engaged couple.

In-House Caterers

Hotels offer these services, as do most country club/golf courses and social club venues. There are several advantages when using an in-house caterer, the biggest being that you don't have to go through the trouble of finding one yourself. In-house caterers are already familiar with the particulars of the event space, which is another perk. Servers are on salary, and hotel professionals have a proven system with a kitchen that they know well. In addition, hotel servers will be able to answer any question your guests may have.

Some reception places with on-site caterers may allow you the option of bringing in another catering service, but with most, it's their service or no venue. If the food is good and the price is reasonable, you may find this arrangement perfect for you.

Off-Site Caterers

Before you go searching for an independent caterer, find out what your reception site provides and what it doesn't. Some offer linens, glasses, dinnerware, tables, chairs (and sometimes everything but the food and beverages). Others provide nothing but the space. Know what you need. Also, check if the venue has a list of preferred or suggested caterers you can start your search with.

SIMPLE OFF-SITE CATERING

Some caterers specialize in keeping it simple. They provide food, period. Everything else like beverages, linens, dinnerware, glasses, and service are left up to you. Sometimes this can work to your advantage. Caterers like these may offer great food at a low price. However, don't be fooled into thinking that this will always mean less money, unless you are serving super-simple fare at your micro wedding. Contracting with a simple caterer only makes sense when you have a very specific type of food in mind that you feel no one else could provide. It could be Aunt Mary, because you love her amazing crab cakes, or that favorite restaurant where you go every Saturday night. No matter how much you love their food, there is the disadvantage of considerably more work for you. What you could be getting in one package from a full-service caterer (which will be covered next), you'll have to handle yourself. If you don't mind making lots of calls (or asking a lot of people to help you), this will be a project to factor into your planning.

You will also need to research businesses that specialize in event rentals. If your reception site doesn't provide tables and chairs, for example, you'll have to find out what you'll need to determine a fair price for the cost of these rentals. Then you'll have to figure out how to get it all to the site on the day of your wedding and return all of it afterward. You will also need to find people who are willing to set things up for you; you will be focusing on getting yourself ready on the wedding day, not hauling chafing dishes and chairs around at the reception site. Of course, the best thing to do is to hire a waitstaff personnel company to provide the waiters and setup crew that you need. In the end, you may end up spending the same amount of money (or more) that you would for a full-service caterer.

FULL-SERVICE OFF-SITE CATERING

Full-service caterers, which most people associate with wedding and event receptions, provide food, beverages, waitstaff, and bartenders. If you need tables, chairs, linens, and tabletop items (china, glassware, flatware, etc.), these caterers will usually do all the legwork for you and simply add that to the cost of your total bill.

If the rental company they are using does not have the exact look you are going for, you can look into another rental company. Rentals are tricky, however, so usually it's best to hire an experienced wedding planner or designer, or ask your floral designer if they have access to other rental companies that could provide the style you have in mind.

Some full-service caterers will let you supply your own alcohol, but some prefer not to worry about the potential liability, depending on your state's laws and their insurance policies. They will not love the loss in revenue either!

The beauty of having your own alcohol delivered from an alcohol distributor or liquor store (if allowed) is that you can often return what is not chilled or opened. Experienced caterers and bartenders know to keep only a certain amount of beer and wine on ice at any given time. Open bottles and chilled items are nonreturnable.

The Selection Process

No matter what type of caterer you decide on, ask questions to make sure they can provide the services you want. Here are some of the main concerns you will have when hiring a caterer for your micro wedding.

1. THE COST

The price of catering can be very complicated. Catering proposals usually include the cost of the food, beverages (both alcoholic and nonalcoholic), rentals, staffing, delivery, and taxes. Caterers can give you an estimate based on the number of guests you plan to have and your menu selections.

> **essential**
>
> Some of your vendors will need to eat at your wedding. Many caterers offer a reduced-price for meals for vendors, so be sure to know the difference in price and let them know the approximate number of vendors who will be staying for the entire evening. Children's meals are often discounted as well.

Ask about price guarantees and substitution pricing in case of serious and unexpected market conditions. Some caterers may also be able to provide staffing for valet and coat check attendants. Always ask if gratuities are included for their staff as well.

2. THE MENU CHOICES

Most experienced caterers will be able to provide a customized menu for your micro wedding. Anything from a cocktail reception to a twelve-course meal with wine pairing is available if you ask for it. The most common styles of catering for weddings are preselected plated meals and buffets. For preselected plated meals, each guest provides their meal choice and any dietary restrictions in their RSVP response. Buffets can be split into stations with themes for a variety of cuisine options. In terms of dessert, many caterers have in-house pastry chefs. If you want to provide a specific type of dessert (or desserts) from another vendor, most caterers are used to that. However, your micro wedding might not be a typical wedding. Most micro weddings are not! Each year new catering trends emerge. Ask your caterer what is on trend during your wedding time frame and evaluate all your options. It's always a good idea to do a little research and ask recent newlyweds for advice on ways to use catering creatively. Your venue manager will know the best caterers that work well for your style. Many venues have preferred caterers, which makes the decision-making process all the easier.

3. THE CONTRACT

When you decide on a caterer that meets your needs, get every verbal agreement in writing. Learn about your caterer's deposit, refund, and postponement policies. Make sure that the vendor lists all the specifics they are providing. Here are the main details to look for in your contract:

- **The date and time of your event.** This should include the day of the week so there is no confusion.
- **Everything that will be provided in your menu.** Make sure that special dietary restrictions, vendor meals, and children's meals are delineated.
- **Who is providing alcohol.** If the caterer is providing alcohol, specific types and brands should be fully identified. Don't accept "domestic and imported beers," as there are thousands of brands. For example, if you want a local

brewery's beer along with a popular national brand and three specific imported brands, be sure that is listed on the contract. If you opt for "top shelf" liquors, be sure to select those brands as well. "Top shelf" almost always means the most expensive, so you should have what you want or at least know what will be provided. Be aware that you may have to pay an additional fee for specific brands.

- **The nonalcoholic options.** Most caterers will provide nonalcoholic beverages at a flat rate per person. Just be sure to know the exact brands they will be serving (you may be partial to specific brands) so you are not disappointed. Also be sure both still and sparkling water are listed (which is standard) along with juices like orange, cranberry, and grapefruit. If children are attending the wedding, you may want to provide grape and/or apple juices as well.

- **All the rentals the caterer will be providing.** You will need to know the sizes of tables; types of chairs; standard (versus upgraded) tabletop items, like linens, glassware, china, and flatware; and what is provided for the bar.

- **The number of servers, kitchen staff, and bartenders who will be working your wedding day.** You may also want to know what the servers will be wearing that day. If you are having a formal occasion, be sure to ask if they will be wearing tuxedos and that it is noted in the contract. If you are having an informal affair and would like the servers to have more of a bistro-style outfit, that should also be discussed and noted. Some caterers have access to more options for their staffing than others. For example, if you want the servers to wear khaki pants and pink aprons to go with your theme, you may have to pay for the aprons. Always ask—they may have what you want at no extra charge!

- **What you will be paying in taxes.** Many caterers use the tactic of not calculating the taxes until after you have signed their contract and the final bill is due. You don't want to be surprised by an extra few hundred or even thousand dollars a week before your wedding.

> **fact**
>
> Be sure that you're allowed to see a sample table setup. Many couples are not ready to make final decisions on rentals at the time they sign their catering contracts. Once you have your color palette and design for the day, set up a time to see the finalized look to ensure it's what you want!

Check out the Appendix at the back of this book for checklists to help you determine and navigate your catering needs.

Wedding Cake and Other Desserts

As discussed earlier, your caterer may provide dessert or allow another vendor to handle this. Desserts can be a signature décor display at micro weddings. Desserts come in all sorts of varieties, so think about what each of you loves individually or something you love to enjoy or even make together. For example, if you love to make cookies together or cookies are your favorite dessert, have a cookie "buffet." Or if doughnuts are your go-to treat, have a doughnut wall. If neither one of you has a sweet tooth, consider having a display of different desserts to entertain your guests. The variety will depend on the number of guests. If close to fifty guests are attending, provide a few different varieties while keeping in mind those guests who may need options free of gluten, dairy, and/or nuts. A good rule of thumb for multiple desserts is to always have at least one type of chocolate dessert, at least one fruit-centric dessert, and at least one vegan/non-dairy/gluten-free dessert depending on the allergies of you and your guests. If you are having fewer than ten guests, why not ask what their favorite desserts are? You may already know! Maybe many of them love chocolate and fruit. Combining the two in a plated dessert course can do the trick. However, if you have guests with allergies, you will want to make sure that you have a special option for them. If you don't know what to do, go with tradition and have a small cutting cake with an extra sheet cake (depending on the number of guests you are having) to keep it simple. Ask your cake designer for advice on the amount of cake you will need for the size of your guest list.

Beverages

No matter what time of year you are having your wedding, or how many people will be there, your guests will be thirsty. The following are the standard alcoholic and nonalcoholic beverages you may want to include on your wedding menu.

Alcoholic Refreshments

Most wedding receptions have some sort of alcohol. If you are having an elopement or are even self-officiating, you may want to have a bottle of champagne to celebrate or bring your favorite beer. Alcohol is totally up to you and not necessarily about what your guests want. Whether you are having three or fifty guests, the amount and types of alcohol will depend on your budget and style (just like everything else). Here are the most common levels of providing alcohol at micro weddings:

- **Just a champagne toast.** It could be you are getting married at the courthouse. Maybe the two of you are meeting a few friends at a bar after your elopement or having a micro wedding at home and just want to pop the cork for a quick toast in celebration. There's no rule that you must drink or provide alcohol at your wedding. However, if a little bubbly is enough for you, it also does not have to break the bank. You don't have to get Dom Pérignon! Opt for a fun sparkling wine and keep it on a budget.
- **Beer and wine.** Many micro wedding couples who are more interested in the style of their event (and are not particularly focused on their bar) will opt for just beer and wine. However, limiting the bar doesn't mean you can't get creative. If you love a local brewery or a particular beer that can come in a keg, why not have a fun beer tap display customized for your wedding? If you love all kinds of beers and want to serve several types of bottled or canned options from around the world, make the display part of the wedding décor. You can showcase beers and wines from the different places you have traveled to if you are having a travel theme, or just share your favorites. Again, here is where a wedding planner or designer can help you get creative in the bar department to really showcase your style, even on a budget! Remember, you will also want to provide wines for your sit-down dinner (if you are having one). Be sure to ask your caterer for advice on what pairs well with the food; you may want to serve something different from what is available at the bar. You can also provide sparkling wine for your toast and leave it at that or have some extra sparkling wine at the bar (like prosecco, cava, brut, and rosé varietals).
- **Signature cocktails.** In addition to beer and wine, many couples will offer a specialty cocktail, which saves money over a

full bar. Specialty cocktails can be pretty much anything that is your favorite! If you are a whiskey sour kind of person and your fiancé loves a Manhattan, consider serving only those two drinks (they normally get served in the same type of glassware too)! Or provide a simple cocktail like sangria or mimosas for a fun theme and to keep things colorful and interesting. Sangrias can be made with white or red wines, and mimosas come in many fruity flavors and colors. Ask your caterer or wedding planner for some fun accents to go along with your specialty cocktail, like customized drink stirrers, cocktail napkins, or garnishes like candied fruit to match your color or theme.

- **Full bar.** A full bar will usually be handled by your caterer. They will provide most of the different types of alcohol along with mixers (triple sec, club soda, tonic, simple syrup, etc.). If you want to learn how to provide alcohol for your own bar DIY-style, check out Chapter 10. In addition to the full bar, you can add specialty cocktails and a champagne toast.

In the end, you can serve whatever you like in terms of alcohol at your wedding. Alcohol not your thing? Skip it, or provide your favorite mocktails! Remember, micro weddings are about your personal style and not necessarily about what the guests want.

YOUR LIABILITY AS HOST

Drinking alcohol is common at a wedding reception. However, wedding guests have been known to go beyond the limits of common sense. Many courts around the world have ruled that hosts, caterers, and restaurants alike are liable when drunken guests from private parties become involved in auto accidents or criminal matters. As a host and loved one, call a taxi, rideshare service, or find someone to drive a drunk guest home or to their hotel after the reception. Also, underage drinking is illegal almost everywhere—

be sure you know the laws of the state or country where the reception takes place. To avoid these situations, discuss with your caterer ways to limit alcohol consumption at your reception when someone seems to be reaching their limit. Additionally, a reputable caterer will always have bartenders who are trained to know when to ask guests for identification to verify they are of legal age. Reliable caterers are happy to cooperate and can suggest options.

Nonalcoholic Refreshments

If you do include alcohol at your micro wedding, be sure to include nonalcoholic options as well. Every bar should stock sodas, iced tea (sweetened or unsweetened), juices, and waters (still and sparkling). You can also include interesting and popular infused sparkling water varieties to fit your style.

In addition to having cold nonalcoholic beverages at the bar, it is always nice to have hot tea and coffee available (both regular and decaffeinated). In fact, impressive and more elaborate coffee stations are very popular at modern weddings—large and micro alike. In most metropolitan areas you can hire a traveling barista coffee vendor with the necessary equipment to whip up hot or cold espresso-based drinks! If not, ask if your caterer has the ability to upgrade their basic coffee station.

> **essential**
>
> Be aware of guests who may be recovering (or active) alcoholics. Think about offering a few fun mocktail options in addition to your specialty cocktails. If you are getting married during a warm season, having a mocktail available is the best way to keep your guests hydrated while adding some fun flair as well!

Checklists for your beverage needs can be found in the Appendix at the back of this book.

Rental Options

Rental options go far beyond catering. Rentals can include entertainment equipment, furniture, tabletop upgrades, décor rentals, specialty cars, and transportation, along with any number of things that spark your personal style. The following sections discuss the most popular (but certainly not all) rental options for meaningful and stylish micro weddings.

Entertainment Equipment

Entertainment rentals are a great way to infuse your style into your wedding day. Here are just a few fun and popular ideas available for rental in most major cities:

- **Carnival equipment.** Fun options include cotton candy machines, popcorn makers, adult bounce houses, and interactive games (like dunking machines) with actors.
- **Outdoor and indoor gaming equipment.** Add some fun with games like cornhole; large Connect 4, Jenga, and Twister games; casino tables; and even vintage arcade games.
- **Photo booths.** Companies have found innovative and interesting ways to let you rent DIY equipment to set up your own booth. Interesting backdrops are available as well.
- **Food trucks, ice cream carts, and specialty bar stations.** These are very popular rentals at weddings. While not necessarily something just to rent (as they need personnel and the concoctions they provide), they can add a really fun vibe by using vehicles like Airstream trailers, VW buses, or pickup trucks.

When it comes to finding rentals, you will want to look to your wedding planner or designer. If you do not have room in your budget for a wedding planner, use local wedding vendor guides and ask your venue manager along with any of your other wedding vendors about their recommendations. Good vendors always know about other good vendors.

Furniture, Upgraded Tabletop, and Décor Rentals

Some of the easiest ways to upgrade your micro wedding are with gorgeous vintage, shabby-chic, antique, or modern furniture. Many of these particular niche/specialty rental companies will also have interesting tabletop and accent décor items for rent as well. If you are looking for an interesting set of colored flatware or fun retro dessert glasses for your vintage ice cream bar, specialty rental companies are the way to go. Some are hard to find and may be available only in certain cities. This is a major aspect of décor and design that can be easily handled logistically with a wedding planner or designer.

Specialty Car and Transportation Rentals

If you are looking for a particular vibe in terms of photography or you are having a much smaller micro wedding or elopement, specialty transportation vehicles may be right up your alley. Looking for that vintage blue Mustang for your portraits? Want to take an airplane ride? Hoping to take your seventeen guests on a trolley ride downtown in your favorite city on earth? Envisioning yourself on a light pink Vespa at your Italian destination wedding? There are specialty vendors and rentals for all of that! Depending on where you live and where you want to get married, you may have any number of options available. This is where micro weddings get super interesting and end up taking you and your guests to places you have not thought of before! Don't know where to find these vendors? A wedding planner will.

Ceremony Music

Carefully selected music provides atmosphere and meaning to your ceremony. You may already have a clear vision of the type of music you want. Depending on the type of ceremony, you may need prelude music, processional music, music during the ceremony, and recessional music.

If you're interested in additional musicians, singers, and songs, consult with the officiant in charge of your ceremony. Some religions place restrictions on secular selections—or any kind of music—during ceremonies, but others may be open to it. Ask about this well in advance of starting your search for ceremony musicians. The following should give you a clearer idea of what kind of music is classic for some of the more common religions around the world.

Church Ceremonies

If you are having your ceremony in a church, use what they have! An organist or a pianist can always do the trick. You can add some pomp and circumstance by adding a trumpet or a harp for your entrance. But if you don't like the idea of traditional hymnal music, ask your pastor if you can bring in a string quartet, classical guitarist, or any number of other instruments and ensembles.

Jewish Ceremonies

Traditional music for Jewish ceremonies can include a cantor to sing the Sheva Brachot (traditional seven blessings) and other songs and chants. The recessionals of most Jewish weddings include a festive ensemble of musical instruments including the clarinet, violin, guitars, and drums, though there could be an accordion and even a full orchestra if you like. The musical style is folksy, stemming from European traditions, which encourages dancing and clapping by the wedding party and the guests.

Muslim Ceremonies

No music is played during the nikkah if it is held in a mosque. Since Islam is a multi-ethnic religion with practitioners from the Middle East, Africa, Iran, and Central and South Asia, musical traditions and expressions differ significantly after the nikkah ends, depending on where the couple (or their families) come from. For example, in Afghanistan, Azerbaijan, parts of Pakistan, Tajikistan, and Uzbekistan, the "Ahesta Bero" is the first song sung or played once the couple has finished the nikkah and are welcomed into the reception.

---

question

Why is my religion or culture not listed?

There are over 4,300 known religions in the world. While each is just as meaningful as the next, several books would be needed to cover ideas for all of them! Find out more about your religion's expectations and culture from your officiant, families, friends, libraries, and online search engines.

There are countless beautiful songs for Islamic wedding receptions. Be sure to ask your parents and extended family for advice.

Hindu Ceremonies

The use of dhol drummers for the groom's *baraat* (entrance) is very popular. Other instruments that can be found at the various stages of an Indian wedding are the sitar (a long, stringed instrument), tabla (a pair of hand drums), and bansuri (a wooden flute). Many couples choose some of these same instruments for certain parts of their cocktail hour or reception.

Chinese Ceremonies

The use of stringed instruments such as the guqin (which translates as "ancient musical instrument"—seven-stringed plucked instrument); erhu (also known as the Chinese violin, with two strings and played with a bow); guzheng (a fifteen- or twenty-five-stringed instrument that is plucked); and pipa (also known as the Chinese lute) is popular. Other traditional instruments include the dizi and xiao, which are both wind instruments.

Japanese Ceremonies

The koto and shamisen are the two most popular Japanese musical instruments used for ceremonies. The koto is a long zither with thirteen woven strings that are plucked and strummed. The shamisen is a skin-covered lute with three woven silk strings that are plucked with a bachi made of ivory.

Persian Ceremonies

A wide range of music can be played during a Persian ceremony. Classical instruments for Persian ceremonies include the setar (not to be confused with a sitar, but also a kind of lute that is plucked), kamāncha (a three- or four-stringed bowed instrument), and santur (a hammered dulcimer played with mallets).

Other Ceremony Music

If you are not religious and/or you don't want to incorporate cultural heritage into your ceremony, have whatever music you want! If your ceremony is in a garden or a ballroom, consider at least one instrument (like an acoustic guitar, violin, or trumpet), or have a DJ or band pipe in music from a speaker. Or you may opt to have a fun trio or a fantastic a cappella group sing for you.

Also, don't worry if you think you don't know enough about classical music (should you choose to hire classical musicians). The musicians can offer suggestions based on guidelines you offer them. On the other hand, if you know exactly what you want and your chosen musicians don't have it in their repertoire, simply buy the music for them. Be sure to send the music to them ahead of time so they can have time to practice! Classical musicians can play modern songs and almost any sort of theme song if you provide the sheet music for it.

Reception Music

Music at the wedding reception is the number one form of entertainment for your guests. Micro weddings may allow enough flexibility in the budget for a band versus a DJ. Remember that the right music adds emotion, drama, and fun to your reception; the wrong music can dampen your reception mood. When hiring a band or a DJ, think through the dancing portion of your event (if you are having any). Can you easily do all of these dances with a fun band, or is there one special song that you really want played as an original recorded piece of music? Bands and DJs both can play recorded music, so don't fret. Whether you are going with a formal or informal wedding reception, the possibilities are endless when it comes to music selection. Typically, a formal micro wedding reception will include a large band or a DJ that plays a mix of songs all generations can enjoy. Formal receptions almost always include several times throughout the reception when couples dance to slower songs. A less formal micro wedding reception will depend on the couple's personal vibe and the music that their guests will want to hear.

Bands

Bands are often the first choice for wedding receptions, if the budget allows for it. The most popular choice is a variety band able to play a wide range of music. You can opt for a band that can represent the musical era or genre you want for a themed reception. You could choose, for example, to have a classical ensemble for your cocktail reception and an eight-piece band for dinner and dancing.

Whichever type of band you choose, there are a number of logistics involved in having a band at your reception. Before you book a band, make sure that the reception site has enough space and sufficient power for it. The last thing you want is a large band and a tiny dance floor! Consult with your venue manager to see how they manage bands with larger electrical needs to get the best advice.

> **alert**
>
> A large band that charges less than a DJ is often a band that rarely plays weddings. Why is this important? Although they may be cheaper, they may not be sensitive to the time constraints of a wedding and the flow of most receptions. Be sure they are ready to take on this challenge and will dress accordingly!

If you have a particular song that you want played during the cocktail hour or a special dance, you can almost always provide music for your band to play from their sound equipment. While bands are not DJs, they are aware that they may not be able to perform every song you want at your wedding (or maybe they have that much range!). If you would like to play recorded multicultural music at certain times at the reception and then switch to live music at other times, let that be known before you sign a contract. Whatever type of band you choose for your reception, keep in mind that they will almost always cost more than a DJ.

There are a few other logistics to keep in mind when you hire a band. Most bands require at least one break and must be fed. A great time for the band to eat is while you are eating, and they can have band members take turns playing while others eat, which makes for a lighter sound during dinner. Or have the band amplify a playlist of your choice through their sound system. The band can also take a break when (and if) you are cutting the cake or doing toasts. However, make sure that there is never a long break without music or other entertainment. A lack of music can give guests the impression that there is an issue or that the reception is over.

DJs

For many couples, a DJ is an easier option than a band. Most reputable and experienced wedding DJs are able to provide a wide range of music for less money than an experienced live band. A DJ can provide a mix of genres to please everyone in your crowd, and they can easily change up the style of music you want as the night goes on. This is especially important as the dancing portion of the evening starts to ramp up. If you are mixing two cultures, you may want to have a DJ who can play music from both of your cultures throughout the night. A talented and prepared DJ will be able to play your favorite radio mixes, "oldies but goodies," important cultural music, and that amazing fight song from your alma mater all in one night (without missing a beat).

Although a DJ does not have the same electrical power needs as a band, you may end up needing additional equipment, like multiple speakers, wireless microphones, and a separate set of sound equipment for your ceremony and cocktail hour. Ask your DJ about pricing on these extras before you sign a contract.

If you are having your ceremony and reception in the same location, it is sometimes easier (and very cost-effective) to go with a DJ as they can play recorded classical or instrumental music for your ceremony along with everything you want for the reception.

Chapter Eight

Photography, Videography, and Online Wedding Components

Photography and videography are standard elements of any wedding, whether traditional or micro. However, online wedding components and social media elements are incredibly important for micro weddings due to the smaller guest count. Sharing your wedding online with people who are unable to attend the big day (or didn't end up on the final guest list) is crucial to most micro wedding couples to ensure no one feels left out. This chapter is full of information on how to record everything that happens on your micro wedding day!

Photography

Modern wedding photography is all about emotions, capturing the little details, the style of the couple, and how the couple interact with each other and their guests the day of the wedding. It's an important way to remember the event for years to come, and to share it with those who could not attend. It is not uncommon for some wedding photographers to offer both digital and film photography. There is a distinct difference between the two, and they both have their merits (which will be covered later in this chapter). However, the micro wedding style of both digital and film wedding photography is generally very emotive and detail oriented.

Finding a photographer for your meaningful micro wedding day is not simply about finding the best-reviewed professionals on some wedding website or *Instagram*. Wedding photographers have distinctive styles, just as your micro wedding will have a distinctive style. They also have a wide range of personalities. Don't just look at a photographer's pricing if you have fallen in love with their website. The price tag drives a lot of couples, but remember that wedding photography is more than just the photos themselves.

> **alert**
>
> Don't take a risk on an unproven entity. Take the time to find a photographer who knows what they are doing. There is no substitute for the education and experience of a professional photographer. There are countless stories of couples that have received less than quality work for their money. Don't become one of these stories!

Photography is the number one way you will preserve the history of your uniting families. It is an investment for future generations in your family as well. Needless to say, you don't want to put this huge responsibility in the hands of just anyone, so be very careful during the selection process. Meeting a photographer is absolutely essential so you can get a grasp of their personality and process.

Most photographers offer packages based on the number of hours you will need for the day of the wedding. In addition, most photographers offer "à la carte" services, including engagement shoots and albums. Choose a package that is right for you and your style. You can, of course, look for the best value, but remember: You will do yourself a big favor by opting to pay a little more for a quality job. The non-monetary cost of having a bad photographer will be considerably more.

fact

A photographer's high price tag does not necessarily mean you'll be getting a great personality on the day of the wedding. A low price tag, however, is a pretty reliable sign that the photographer has less experience. This is one wedding expense that really is worth the research and money that it requires.

In most cases a good photographer will have an extensive website with galleries of the weddings, portraits, experiences, and events that they have shot in addition to albums that they prepared for prospective clients. Many experienced photographers are a part of various organizations like WPPI (Wedding and Portrait Photographers International) and WPJA (Wedding Photojournalist Association), which means they are actively involved in educating themselves and possibly others. As technology rapidly changes every day, so does photography. Again, an educated and experienced photographer is your best bet!

If you can find several photographers that meet your criteria, narrow the choices by looking at personality. Keep in mind your photographer is with you *all* day long on your wedding day. You want to make sure you like them and can be comfortable with them. Your photographer will be taking photos of you while you are getting dressed and while you kiss after saying "I do." Don't you want that person to feel like a friend or even family that day?

Second Shooters versus Assistants

When hiring a photographer, ask if they will charge for an additional second shooter or an assistant. A second shooter is not the same as an assistant. A second shooter is exactly that: a second professional photographer at your wedding.

alert

Obviously, a second photographer means a higher price tag. You and your partner need to decide on the importance of a second shooter based on your style and the type of photographer you choose. A side note: Not all photographers feel comfortable with a second shooter.

A second shooter is needed for larger weddings and large wedding parties along with multiple locations for photo opportunities. If your micro wedding is being shot in multiple locations and you want the pre-ceremony aspects of getting dressed and details of the day to be photographed, a second shooter may be important for you (especially if you are having your ceremony and reception in two different locations). Another big reason why some couples choose to have a second shooter is that they are interested in having high-end staged, dramatic, and moody portraiture in multiple locations. If you are really into fashion and the details of the day, the second shooter can be at the reception taking detail shots while the main photographer is shooting your portraits. However, since micro weddings have a shorter guest list and smaller wedding parties, you need to discuss with your photographer of choice their process and need for a second shooter (and if they think it is necessary alongside your timeline).

An assistant, on the other hand, does not take photos that day. They help the photographer get the lenses that they need and carry their bags around all day, as well as help with lighting and positioning you and details in the wedding. The assistant is not usually an experienced photographer, although they may be. Many assistants are interns "learning the ropes" of professional photography.

Sometimes a photographer brings an assistant who is also an experienced shooter, and you will reap the benefits. How does this happen? Photographers know a lot of other photographers, and sometimes they need an extra hand if you're having a super-detailed wedding. They may actually be excited about your wedding and want a second pair of eyes from an experienced photographer they trust.

Another reason to bring a second shooter is that photographers are human. They have a contract with you, but maybe they have had a hard week. Maybe they've been ill, or someone they love passed away recently. Whatever the reason, they may just need extra help on your wedding day. This is the case with all your vendors. They understand that this is one of the most important days of your life. Experienced wedding photographers know that a micro wedding is a very emotional and meaningful wedding. They also know that you don't get that day back and you're depending on them to provide quality images.

Usually you'll pay for a second photographer to shoot your wedding but not for an assistant.

Questions for Your Photographer

Don't be afraid to ask your photographer questions (they are used to it). Here are some things you'll want clarified before hiring them:

- How long have they been in business?
- Have they taken photos at your ceremony and reception sites?
- Are they a full-time photographer?
- What kinds of packages do they offer?
- What is their hourly fee for additional hours?
- Do you own the images after the wedding, or do you have to wait a certain period of time?

Be sure to get answers to your questions *before* you sign a contract with a photographer.

Things to Look For

There's more to this than asking questions, of course. Since you may not have experience working with professional photographers, the following are key things to look out for when hiring a photographer for your micro wedding.

> **essential**
>
> Some photographers make income during the off-season, when not many weddings are scheduled. Don't be surprised if a wedding photographer has a section in their portfolio devoted to non-wedding portraits. You just need to see that they are full-time photographers.

Steer clear of part-time photographers who only occasionally handle weddings. They're not likely to have the equipment and experience of an expert in the field, and their lack of commitment to this line of work will often show in the final product. You want a full-time wedding photographer, not someone who does this as a hobby. This is your wedding day.

If you're planning on working with a photography studio, choose one that specializes in weddings. Only experienced wedding professionals know all the nuances of photographing a wedding—how to avoid problems, when to fade into the background, and the best way to compose a great portrait in natural light (or with additional lighting if needed).

> **alert**
>
> Avoid large online studios that appear to use an assembly-line approach. They often subcontract photographers and normally won't guarantee which photographer will show up on your wedding day. You need more than just a warm body as a photographer on your wedding day.

If you find a studio you like, ask to see sample wedding images that were taken by the same photographer who will be working your wedding. If the studio can't or won't supply them, find another one to work with. A high-quality studio or photographer will take three times as many photos as you signed on for, to give you the best and broadest selection.

Digital versus Film

Although the days of shooting weddings with film only are starting to fade, there are still photographers that use both DSLRs (digital single-lens reflex cameras) and traditional film SLRs (single-lens reflex). The majority of wedding photographers use DSLRs; some photographers still love to use film-based SLR cameras, and some even like to use the twin-lens reflex (TLR) for medium-format photography. They like these various styles of cameras for artistic and photography purist reasons (and you may too)!

> **essential**
>
> The medium-format TLR is fun and artistic. Have your photographer use it if you want a vintage, old-fashioned feel to your wedding and you don't have a very strict timeline. Or use it just for a photo booth for your guests during the reception!

A DSLR camera is the best choice for most wedding photographers for its ease of use, but if your photographer likes to mix it up between a TLR and a DSLR, let them do so. The more artistic your photographer is, the better and more interesting photos they will produce. Just keep in mind that this may cost more money and will most likely eat up a little more time.

Photojournalistic versus Traditional

There are two camps of wedding photography to consider in addition to the style and personality of a photographer: photojournalistic style and traditional style.

PHOTOJOURNALISTIC STYLE

A photojournalistic-style photographer will take photos as the wedding day unfolds naturally and without much interruption. The photographer's job here is to tell the story of your wedding day without playing any role in it. They are an observer who captures images. Photojournalistic wedding photography is all about producing real, raw, authentic photos that show the facts of the day (think newspaper style). There are distinct advantages and disadvantages to this style of wedding photography.

The advantages are:

■ Your album will look like the story of your wedding day.
■ Photos tend to look natural and "unposed."
■ Without posed photography, there tends to be less stress of herding wedding parties.

The disadvantages are:

■ There are few or no family portraits.
■ There is an incredible amount of unpredictability.
■ You may not always have the most flattering images of you and your family.

The majority of couples today are choosing this style (also known as documentary style) of photography for their weddings.

TRADITIONAL STYLE

Most modern couples choose the photojournalistic style for their wedding photography, but plenty of couples prefer traditional style. Traditional wedding photography is all about planned and posed photos; the photographer exerts lots of control. There is a definite photography timeline, schedule, and detailed list of photographs that must be taken with lots of direction and lots of lighting. If your photos require a ton of setup and time, they're traditional photography. Like photojournalistic photography, traditional photography has its own advantages and disadvantages.

The advantages are:

- Your family will be elated to have all of the posed family portraits that they now don't have to pay for.
- With planning, there is a certain amount of control.

The disadvantages are:

- Posed images tend to be very time-consuming and stressful for all of the people involved in the posing and the timeline of the day.
- Not everyone is comfortable posing for the camera, and the pictures will look staged, not authentic to real life.

In reality, most weddings have a mix of photojournalistic style with a dash of traditional to keep all parties happy. Let the photographers you are interviewing know what style you want for your wedding day, whether it is one style or the other or a little bit of both. A good photographer will hopefully be flexible.

Photo List

Should you decide to go with at least a little traditional photography for your wedding day, you will need to sit down with your photographer and discuss your wants, needs, and expectations for your posed photos. Let your photographer know the special things that you've always dreamed of for your wedding photos. If you want only posed family photos, then leave it at that. If you want the reception photographed, let them know. Give your photographer a list of all the special people you want included in the pictures, especially anyone who isn't in the wedding party. Your photographer may be exceptional, but they are not a mind reader. If your eighty-year-old aunt is famous for dancing at family functions, make sure to tell the photographer that you want that moment captured on camera.

Formal Photos Before the Wedding

Although it's considered "bad luck" for couples to see each other before the ceremony, many micro wedding couples feel comfortable taking the formal shots before the wedding. This makes life easier for a lot of people. The photographer doesn't have to rush to get all the shots on your list during the cocktail hour, and you get to enjoy more of that hour. If seeing your fiancé before the ceremony is absolutely out of the question for you, try to take as many of the formal pictures as you can without your fiancé. For example: you alone, you and your parents, you and your attendants, and so on. At the reception, speed things up by making sure everyone who's going to be in a portrait knows where they are supposed to be and when.

Special Locations

Some couples opt to take their formal wedding photos at a special location other than the reception site. Sometimes it's a place with great sentimental value, a historical landmark, or just somewhere with gorgeous scenery. If you do plan to take your photo shoot on the road, just remember that your guests will have to wait longer than usual to see you (and their dinner) at the reception.

Videography

Ironically, newlyweds are the people who usually remember the least about their wedding. They're in a fog of emotion and excitement, in which hundreds of sensory impressions go by in a blur. Still photographs will show you staged poses and moments in time, but video will show events in action. When a couple finally gets the chance to watch their video, it certainly brings back memories, but it also shows them many things they hadn't seen before. Don't leave videography to a friend or a relative unless you've seen a sample of their work and were impressed by it. Your fiancé's brother may have the best intentions and even own a good video camera, but odds are he won't have the necessary sound and editing equipment to make a professional-style video for you. He may also miss some key moments while he is trying to enjoy the party himself!

---

question

Where should I start searching for a videographer?
If you're working with an independent photographer or a studio for your wedding photography, they should be able to recommend videographers. Other resources include recent newlyweds, venues, and your wedding planner!

When searching for a videographer, apply the same basic guidelines you would for photographers. Images should be crisp and clear, and the colors true to life. You want to be comfortable with your videographer and confident that they won't be ordering your guests in and out of shots. Also ask about editing capabilities, wireless mics, and lights. Find out how many cameras they have and how many people will be assisting on the job, as well as the costs associated with each individual. Ask to view recent sample videos. You're looking for smooth editing, clear sound, and an overall professional cinematic look and feel to the video.

With all of the technology available today, you don't have to settle for anything short of cinematography-quality production values. When looking for a videographer, you can tell the difference between a novice and an experienced professional by the quality of the audio and use of excessive lighting in video samples.

Adding an Online Component

With the invention of the iPad and other devices that use a cell tower, weddings were forever changed. Some people will just not be able to make it to your wedding, whether it is due to budget, health/safety reasons, or simply because you want a smaller wedding. Having a micro wedding means you may want to plan for an online component for those unable to attend the day. Of course, you don't have to include this element in your micro wedding if you don't want to. That is totally understandable. Micro weddings, after all, are known for being intimate and for some that means more privacy. However, if you do want others to join in on the ceremony (or the entire day), there are some really great ways to plan your micro wedding in such a way that makes it inclusive of those who are online with you.

Send the Micro Wedding to Them!

If the pandemic of the 2020s has shown us anything, it's that there's no limit to what you can do at home! Why not send the micro wedding to your virtual guests in fun and interesting ways? There are countless ways to get online attendees more involved. The following are of some of the more popular among micro wedding couples.

To make this super intentional, be sure to send your virtual guests actual invitations in the mail with instructions on how to be an online participant at your wedding. You can also send a magnet reminder for their refrigerator!

HAVE YOUR ONLINE GUESTS DRESS UP

The most popular way to get your online guests involved is to have them dress up for the occasion. While some guests might find it silly to put on their finery if they can't actually be present, some will find it a really fun way to feel like a part of your day from a distance. You can even let them know the theme of your day (if you have one) or the color palette so they can dress accordingly. Some may even go as far as to rent a tux or buy a new dress for the occasion! Why not? They would if they were actually going to be present at your wedding.

LET THEM COOK

Another fun way to help your online participants be part of the wedding day is to have your caterer send care packages and instructions on how to cook your wedding menu at home. The care package would include some of the nonperishable ingredients that will be cooked with the main entrée, along with a note of the perishable ingredients that they would need to purchase locally for the meal. Your online participants have likely had practice—how many people did online cooking classes and Zoom dinner parties during the pandemic? Your micro wedding should feel inclusive to your online guests, and what better way than a shared meal?

You might ask your caterer if they would allow your guests to Zoom or FaceTime into their kitchen while they are prepping food for your wedding day. Seeing the prep work could be incredibly meaningful to some of your food-loving online guests! You can even pay your caterer to do a private online cooking class before the big day (with you and your fiancé present) to help everyone get pumped up and prepped for your micro wedding day. There are any number of ways to make this work.

> **essential**
>
> Have a chef friend of yours cook or bake something that will actually be served at the wedding. That person can deliver the food to the venue and see you before the wedding ceremony begins. This is an easy way to include someone special on your micro wedding day! Just be sure it is okay with your caterer.

LET THEM EAT CAKE (OR DESSERTS)

If you plan on serving an actual wedding cake, ask your baker to provide cupcakes (or mini wedding cakes) to be shipped to your online guests. Of course, if you plan on having another type of dessert instead of cake, you can send anything either locally or via shipping companies. Shippers have come up with innovative ways to mail any type of perishable food—even ice cream! If you are having a dessert display, send virtual guests two of each item you are going to display.

SEND THEM A COCKTAIL KIT

If you plan on serving a signature cocktail or mocktail for your cocktail hour, why not send all the ingredients to your online guests with a pretty printed recipe card and photo representation? An example of a fun, easy cocktail to ship is a ginger mojito. A mojito requires just white rum, fresh mint leaves, sugar, soda water, and lime juice. Adding some ginger to the mix will be a new twist for most people. Include a fun piece of glassware that matches the photo. You can even ask your caterer to produce a simple video on how to make the drink for you to share with online guests or post on social media. Be careful that you pay attention to liquor laws in terms of shipping.

Keep in mind that not everyone drinks alcohol. It will be less expensive, easier to send, and considerate to ship ingredients for a fun mocktail to those guests who don't drink alcohol. A great example for a summer/tropical wedding vibe is to include fruit juice, fruit (with instructions on how to cut the fruit for a fun garnish), and soda water. You know your virtual guest list better than anyone, and you can certainly send different types of beverage ideas to different individuals.

INCLUDE THEM IN YOUR FAVORS LIST

If you are providing favors for your wedding guests on your wedding day, your online guests will appreciate the thought, especially if it is something customized for them specifically. When it comes to favors for those not able to attend the wedding, you always want to go with something that matches the theme of your wedding and your personality—and is also easy to ship. If you have a travel theme, for example, why not send personalized passport holders? Having a wine tasting with your dinner? Send some personalized coasters. Getting married in a coastal town that makes the best saltwater taffy? Send a package of your favorite flavors.

SEND THEM FLOWERS (OR PLANTS)!

Flowers and plants make people happy: It has been scientifically proven! Depending on where your online guests are located, maybe you can send them the same centerpiece that you will be using on the tables on your wedding day. Or if you are using plants as décor, why not send them a plant to let them know you are thinking of them? Be sure to explain to them how you are using the same type of flower or plant for your wedding day.

Social Media

It's only natural that many couples use social media as a means of staying connected to others on their wedding day. Beyond enabling online streaming of the event itself (see more on this in Chapter 3), social media provides an easy way to involve everyone you care about, and there are countless ways to use any platform. However, one thing that is important to consider is privacy. If you really want to keep your micro wedding intimate and private, don't allow social media to be part of your day.

Keeping the day private can be a challenge. Most guests will likely have a smartphone at your wedding and will want to take photos and videos. But you do have the right to privacy on your wedding day. You can include a note in your invitation that your wedding is going to be free of social media, and post a sign at the entrance to the ceremony to remind guests of that fact. Politely requesting privacy for your ceremony and your reception is a normal and perfectly reasonable thing to ask. Most people will be fine with leaving their phones tucked away or just taking their own personal photos and not posting them on social media.

On the flip side, you may want a social media free-for-all. The easiest way to share your photos and videos and to crowdsource all the images and videos that might be produced by your guests on various social media sites is to create a personal hashtag. A hashtag allows you to see everything that gets posted. If there is something that you see later (or during the reception) that you don't want to be on social media, you can politely ask that individual to take the image or video down. Here are the popular social media and other online platforms that couples use in their wedding:

1. **Facebook.** Many micro wedding couples have used *Facebook* to create secret or private group pages to invite both online and actual wedding guests. In these groups, the couple and friends can post notes, photos, and videos. *Facebook* pages end up being a private online scrapbook or "guestbook" for the wedding. Many micro weddings have done away with a physical guestbook in favor of this option. Having a page on *Facebook* is an easy way to keep things private from the world but also accessible to the people you want to share your day with. It is also an easy way to post a quick photo of the two of you just after getting married.
2. **Instagram.** *Instagram* has been the platform of choice for photo crowdsourcing and using hashtags for weddings. *Instagram* also has various capabilities for online videos as well with its "Reels" and "IGTV" features.
3. **Twitter.** While *Twitter* has not been as popular as the previous platforms in terms of wedding online elements, it is one of the most widely used means for disseminating information quickly. It's also another great way to post a photo of the two of you after the ceremony as a wedding announcement.
4. **TikTok.** TikTok is a popular app used for video sharing. Many couples use TikTok to post fun videos leading up to their weddings and also for crowdsourcing videos from their guests during the reception with hashtags.
5. **WhatsApp.** This social media app is hugely popular for international destination weddings. Long-distance calls from one country to another can be expensive. WhatsApp works around that issue by using Wi-Fi connections in any country around the world for free video calling. It is a great way to livestream your wedding for those unable to attend the actual day.

6. **Pinterest.** *Pinterest* is the number one search engine for find-ing ideas for micro weddings. It is another way you can create a secret or public board for your micro wedding as well. Many couples choose to use *Pinterest* boards to show their brides-maids and groomsmen the color palettes and mood for the wedding day. You can also create a secret *Pinterest* board for your online guests to gather ideas for what they can expect. Use pins to show your online guests your color palette, spe-cialty cocktail recipes, and possible outdoor games you might be playing on your wedding day. If you have creative, willing, and fun online guests, you never know what they might drum up for your wedding day and post on social media!

Be sure to have a conversation with your partner about social media being involved in your wedding. Make a decision that you can both feel comfortable with.

Chapter Nine

Showers and Other Parties

Like any other wedding, micro weddings include showers and parties! Micro weddings have a special caveat, though, when it comes to parties outside of a wedding shower: You can have a party before or after the wedding day that extends an invitation to those who are not actually invited to the wedding—even if that does cause the entire brigade of wedding etiquette rule makers throughout history to turn in their graves. Micro weddings are all about throwing caution and tired standards to the wind to enjoy a wedding (and wedding parties!) that focus on what you actually want. This chapter explores each type of micro wedding party in more detail.

Engagement Parties

Once you have told your parents and the world that you are engaged, you can have an engagement party. Usually the bride's parents serve as hosts. However, in recent years it has become more appropriate to ask either set of parents if they would like to throw an engagement party. Couples may even have multiple engagement parties to include family members and friends from different countries, states, and cities. Many couples choose to have a formal engagement party with family and family friends and then to throw a more casual get-together for their inner circle of friends. If both sets of parents want to throw an engagement party and your close friends want to as well, go for it! Being engaged is something to celebrate, and if the logistics make it difficult to have just one or two engagement parties, that is perfectly okay. Just remember that you'll have opportunities to invite people to various types of wedding-related parties, as you will see throughout this chapter. Read through the entire chapter before you make a decision about engagement parties.

Wedding Showers

Wedding showers are a tradition dating back to at least the sixteenth century. People around the world host these pre-wedding parties! And they aren't exclusive to brides.

> **fact**
>
> February 12, 2004, was the first legally gay wedding in the United States. The first recognized legally gay wedding in the world was in Amsterdam on April 1, 2001.

It is important to note that many LGBTQIA+ couples were having commitment ceremonies well before the twenty-first century, and they had wedding showers as well. To recognize this, the traditional term *bridal shower* has been replaced with the term *wedding shower*. Showers can be all-inclusive and can include both sides of the aisle. Have your fiancé come too, if you want! Couples showers are popular. Many couples are getting married later in life, and many are already living together and have established a home. To reflect this, modern showers are less about filling up your home with essentials and more about what you actually need or want.

It will be up to your host to choose who to invite. Be sure, as a couple, that you make the choice as to the type of shower you want. It's likely that several friends and family members will want to host a shower for you. Choose your hosts wisely and make sure each person knows the two of you well enough (especially if you hate shower games!).

Invitations can be done via snail mail or via email/digitally. If you are having an in-person gathering, allow your guests ample notice, especially if you have guests who are traveling from out of town. If you are on a short schedule for your wedding, you can send the invitations out closer to the date if needed.

> **alert**
>
> Invitations should go out about four to six weeks prior to any shower, depending on whether your shower will be virtual or in person. For a virtual shower, four weeks in advance is more than enough time to send an invitation.

When planning a micro wedding, the traditional rules of etiquette sometimes butt up against reality. Do what you want and need to do from a timeline perspective (and for your sanity). If you simply do not have the time for a shower, politely decline if anyone offers to throw you one and thank them graciously.

Couples Showers

Couples showers are great for couples who are already living together and are looking for more nontraditional ways of celebrating. Couples showers give both sides of the aisle a chance to invite their closest friends, but be careful that it does not turn out to be another wedding altogether! The guest list for each shower should be smaller than the guest list for the wedding day. From a micro wedding perspective, couples showers allow hosts to throw you a shower with guests who may not be invited to the wedding due to the smaller guest list. You may find that some of your coworkers or extended family want to throw you a shower so they can celebrate with you too! For many micro weddings, showers end up being a way to involve all the important people in your lives.

However, you should not ask anyone who is not invited to the wedding day to throw you a shower. The subject will come up naturally in conversations about your wedding if you have an extensive list of people who want to celebrate with you. Don't be offended if they don't want to host!

The following are a few of the more popular showers that hosts organize for couples.

HONEYMOON SHOWER

Many couples are getting married later in life and already have a home together. The honeymoon and the wedding day are what they tend to want to focus on in terms of gifts. At websites like HoneyFund.com, you can register for guests to fund your wedding day or honeymoon, or help toward a down payment on a new home (or any savings goal that the two of you are working toward).

While your registry may be geared toward funding your honeymoon, the shower can be all about things you might need while you travel. Some great examples are websites where you can combine bathing suits with lingerie (for a tropical honeymoon) or hiking boots with portable tents (for an adventurous honeymoon) in addition to the honeymoon fund. Some people will feel uncomfortable giving money and really want to give you something you can remember them by. The honeymoon shower is a great way to let them do that! Let your host gather all your ideas and different websites where you have registered for honeymoon gifts, from personalized refillable water bottles on *Etsy* all the way to jewelry you want to wear on that swanky Paris getaway. With a creative host and a carefully curated list of honeymoon needs, this option is perfect for many micro wedding couples. Beyond the gifts, there are all sorts of fun things you can do for a honeymoon shower. You can make your invitations look like boarding passes! You can have a specialty cocktail or cuisine that clearly represents where you are going for your honeymoon. You can turn it into a movie night with your friends where you watch a documentary or a fun film about where you are going for your honeymoon.

CHARITY SHOWER

Many micro wedding couples have it all and don't want gifts for their wedding. A shower may sound frivolous to you, but you can turn it into something unique. At a charity shower, the host helps you plan a day of volunteering coupled with a list of charities you love. Your host can suggest that guests support the charities of your choice and then invite them to a volunteering location. The shower can end with a shared celebration meal if you plan to do the event in person.

This type of shower can also be done virtually. You'll spend time together online with your guests to share with them why volunteering is so important to you and how they can volunteer. This type of virtual shower works really well if you have people all over the country (or world) who want to participate. The two of you will know where each of your guests live, and you can help the host drum up ideas of where each individual guest can volunteer in their respective location! Just be sure to give each guest at least three volunteering options, and try to find ways for them to volunteer not just for the charities that you love but also in ways you think they might love too. Another way this works well is if you send the information off to each individual and give them a reasonable time frame to complete the volunteering task. The shower itself can be a time for everyone to come together online to share their experiences and what it meant to them. You can even ask them to send you a few photos ahead of time to have a video montage of what everyone did! Micro weddings are all about a day with the people you love the most. What greater experience is there to help your guests (and others who might not be invited on the wedding day) connect to the two of you on a deeper level?

ADVENTURE AND EXPERIENCE SHOWER

This type of shower has also become very popular for couples who do not want gifts. Having an interesting experience with your friends before the wedding day is an amazing way to bond and enjoy yourselves instead of getting "showered" with gifts you don't want. Maybe you want to go hiking or camping in the great outdoors. Other outdoor adventure activities you can do for your shower include:

- Taking surf lessons (and maybe even making it into a weekend getaway on a Caribbean island to do so!)
- A golfing weekend
- Skiing at your favorite resort
- A yoga weekend retreat
- Running a marathon or 10K together
- A mountain or lake cabin getaway complete with outdoor activities
- A fishing trip
- Horseback riding
- Taking pilot lessons
- Skydiving
- Bungee jumping
- Glamping (where you have a large tent with flooring, décor, and an actual bed—no sleeping bags here!)
- A beach getaway
- A scavenger hunt

Other experiences that are not necessarily related to sports or the outdoors include:

- Seeing a play on Broadway or at your local theater
- Learning how to make beer or visiting a local brewery, winery, or distillery
- Learning how something you love is made (like a visit to a cacao farm or to see a skateboard designer in action)
- Painting or taking an art class
- A virtual reality experience (Love Star Wars? Try an experience where you get to feel like you are working to escape the Death Star!)
- A murder mystery escape room

- A board game tournament
- A cooking class with a celebrity chef either in person or virtually
- Singing at a karaoke night
- Attending a concert or stand-up comedy show
- A guided tour of a museum

HE SHED/SHE SHED SHOWER

If you happen to be particularly crafty or handy, why not have a power tool or crafting supply shower? If that is what you two love to do together, it is the perfect way to fill your He or She Shed! He Sheds and She Sheds are all about having a small workshop for you on your property. If it is a He Shed, it could look like a typical workshop space or it could be a small workshop for any number of hobbies that a groom might be interested in. If it is a She Shed, it could also be a typical workshop space, but it could be all about crafting or any other hobby a bride might have.

You can create a wish list at various stores and places online and the host can be creative and host the party at your house so the guests can envision or create the shed from scratch, or see the vision that you already have. If it is a specific project that you were hoping to create, maybe your local hardware store has a class that they offer for it. You can also get in touch with a local handyperson or locally owned construction company to have an informal introduction to how to build a shed and use the space efficiently. Another possibly is to contact a local closet designer or feng shui consultant who can help creative energy flow inside the space. The possibilities are endless.

Themed Showers

Many interesting themed showers are popular. If you have a number of friends and/or family members who like to throw parties, you may be one of the lucky few who get to have multiple themed showers! The following are a few traditional and popular shower themes.

KITCHEN THEME

If you are a traditionalist and love to cook and bake, then tradition it is. This shower theme is a classic. At most traditional showers for cooking and baking, there is a time where you will be opening gifts straight from your registry. You can also have the host get creative and livestream a local chef teaching you how to make a certain dish. Just keep it simple and cost-effective so all the guests don't get overwhelmed. It's also a great way to learn more about how the two of you will cook together (if it's a couples shower). Be sure to do your research about what you really want for your kitchen. For example, if you are Italian and have always wanted to learn how to make pasta, experiment by taking a class before adding bulky pasta-making equipment to your registry. You may find your dreams of making pasta every Wednesday night were somewhat misguided, and you don't enjoy doing all that work.

LINGERIE SHOWER

This is one of the most popular shower themes for brides and is the best way to fill your honeymoon suitcase. Don't be shy here! Your friends will want to give you the nicest and sexiest (and maybe even naughtiest) lingerie finds. Be sure to tell them the correct sizes for each item on your registry so you don't have to ask for the receipt later. However, it does not hurt to remind your host to tell the guests to include the receipt with the gift, just in case! This type of shower is done among friends you trust, in a private setting.

GARDEN SHOWER

If one of you has a green thumb, this shower is the perfect way to stock up your gardening shed and plan the garden of your dreams. Have fun researching and planning your dream garden when creating your registry if you have not started an actual garden yet. Some couples wait years before planning their gardens as wedding planning, careers, and babies can take up a lot of your time during the first few years of marriage. Having a head start, you can create a true oasis for your home for entertaining and self-love purposes! Many garden showers are done in your future garden or in someone else's garden. The host may gather plants for your garden or hire a local landscaper to give you a few tips in an outdoor instructional space.

SELF-CARE/SELF-LOVE SHOWER

Another popular shower is the self-care or self-love shower. This type of event became popular after several recent studies sparked a conversation about and awareness of mental health issues. The acceptance that self-care and positive mental health is one of the most important components of daily life gave rise to showers that highlight positive self-care and self-love. If this is a topic that you are interested in as a couple, this can also be a couples shower too. A lot of interesting and meaningful gifts and conversations come out of these showers, which is a great springboard for a healthy marriage.

A few examples of how this shower itself might flow may include activities you want to try and a self-care consultant to guide you through them. Activities such as yoga, Reiki, reflexology, massage therapy, and learning about various self-care apps are popular options. Most self-care consultants are someone like a life coach, personal style/image consultant, holistic health professional, feng shui consultant, or a mental health practitioner. A professional can talk through some simple things that everyone at the shower can engage in to lean in toward a more positive outlook and focus on looking and feeling your best.

ART SHOWER

If you or your partner are artsy or creative, why not have an art shower? This type of party can be for any side of the aisle and can also be a couples shower. You can choose the guest vibe and also the medium(s)! If painting is your preferred art form, have your host bring in an art therapist and teacher to guide you and your guests in a painting class. Or maybe you've been waiting for the chance to set up your dream art studio. This is the perfect opportunity. Just let your host know what supplies you need. This shower could take place at an art studio or in the host's home if they have the space and tools needed for your medium. Who knows, this could inspire your next big career move!

MUSIC SHOWER

If you or your fiancé is a music aficionado, have a music shower! You can also turn this into a couples shower if you both love music. This event can be anything from a shower with a registry of really cool albums you have been pining for or it can be all about getting the equipment to finally set up a music studio for your band. If music is your thing, ask your host if they would be willing to get musically creative with you by asking your guests to bring their own instruments or bring in a music instructor to teach guests how to play a few notes. Or make the shower a musical experience by going to a music class, local concert, or jazz club followed by a meet-and-greet with the musician(s).

BOOK/LIBRARY SHOWER

If you are a book lover, why not have a book shower with your favorite people to spark the book club you've always dreamed of? Choose the book you want to discuss during the shower. For your registry, create a list of the books you have been craving lately to start (or expand) your home library!

FLORAL DESIGN PRACTICE SHOWER

This is the type of shower that couples have when they decide to go DIY for their wedding flowers. Hire a local florist to do a floral design class for you and your bridesmaids or groomsmen. If your maid of honor or best man wants to host this shower, they can take care of the meal, dessert, and beverages. If you want to DIY your flowers for your wedding, this is the perfect way to support a local event floral designer and learn how to avoid mistakes for your actual micro wedding day.

> **essential**
>
> It is important to know that if you end up trying to DIY your flowers and you don't have the proper knowledge, your flowers could die at/before the big day. Some flowers turn brown if you touch the petals, and some flowers don't live very long.

Think of this shower as a trial run to see if you actually have what it takes to design everything for your wedding day. Then, if you think you only want to take care of your centerpieces or scrap the DIY decision altogether after this experience, you can hire the same floral designer to produce the desired designs for your wedding day! You can read more about the details of doing DIY flowers for your wedding day in Chapter 10.

Bachelor and Bachelorette Parties

Though many aspects of weddings have evolved and some traditions are slowly fading, the bachelor and bachelorette party is certainly not going away anytime soon. While some of these parties can be the stuff you see in movies, your party can be a time to do whatever you want. Usually, the best man or maid/matron of honor will throw this party for you. For modern parties, the best man/maid of honor asks exactly what the groom(s)/bride(s) wants to do for their bachelor/bachelorette party. The list of possible activities is endless. Maybe you have always wanted to learn salsa dancing, or you want to go to Miami and just chill on the beach with your best friends. Or perhaps you want an outdoorsy experience like a hiking trip or skydiving. The main point of this party should be about spending time with the people in your life who mean the most to you, doing something you enjoy. They want you to have fun and share memories that will last a lifetime for this party or weekend. So, whether it is an actual party where you hang out somewhere or a full weekend trip, let your best man or maid of honor know clearly what you were hoping to do and what you really hope will *not* happen. Look through the list of adventure showers earlier in this chapter to get the ideas flowing for this party as well.

Rehearsal Dinner

Having a rehearsal dinner is the best way for both sides of the aisle to come together and get to know one another a little better before the wedding day. Most wedding ceremony rehearsals are done the day before the wedding and the rehearsal dinner is done immediately after the actual ceremony rehearsal.

For many micro wedding couples in the United States, a rehearsal and/or rehearsal dinner may go by the wayside, depending on the number of guests who will attend the wedding itself. In most other countries around the world, rehearsals are typically not done, and many couples end up having a fun welcome party the night before their weddings instead (see more in the next section of this chapter). However, in the United States (especially weddings with close to fifty guests), couples often do have a rehearsal and rehearsal dinner for the wedding party (and maybe for out-of-town guests as well). In Western culture, the parents of the groom traditionally host the rehearsal dinner. However, many modern couples and their families, as well as couples and families in other parts of the world, come together to host the rehearsal dinner depending on their budgets.

Welcome Reception

The welcome reception has become wildly popular for micro weddings. Most welcome receptions are held at someone's home, a local restaurant, or the bar or a large suite in the hotel where the majority of your out-of-town guests will be staying. The idea behind this reception is to create time for people from out of town and from both sides of the aisle to meet each other for the first time.

You may want to make this a less formal and more relaxed occasion, especially if you are having a destination wedding, since many guests may arrive just before the welcome reception starts and will be tired from their journey. If you have the welcome reception at a place that is not in the actual venue where the majority of your guests are staying, make sure it is not far from it. There is nothing worse for an out-of-town guest than having to trek an hour away from their hotel accommodations after having been on a plane or having driven for hours to arrive.

In Western culture, the parents of the bride traditionally host the welcome reception. This reception usually involves light refreshments (hors d'oeuvres and drinks). However, many couples decide to host this on their own before or after the rehearsal dinner. Most welcome receptions don't last more than two to three hours.

Wedding Day versus Wedding Weekend

When it comes to micro weddings, you may choose to host a full wedding weekend instead of simply a single wedding day. This entire book is, of course, centered around how to plan your micro wedding day. However, some couples have out-of-town guests who may never have been to the location where you are getting married before. You can always go the traditional route of having just the welcome reception, rehearsal dinner, wedding day, and brunch. Or you can add fun excursion-type activities to the list of events and let others know ahead of time of the options available. This is especially common with destination weddings in foreign countries.

---

alert

It is important to note that if you do end up booking tours in other countries, make sure you are working with a reputable company. Whether you are attending the excursion or just suggesting it to guests, the company leading it should be licensed and insured in case of an accident.

And if you are having your wedding locally but in a city popular for tourism, it's common to curate a fun activity for guests. If your city has great sightseeing activities like museums, beaches, theme parks, sports arenas, historical landmarks, or interesting shopping districts, ask your out-of-town guests what they would like to do. You don't have to participate in any of these tourism activities if it seems like too much is going on already. You don't have to pay for them either.

If you are having your wedding close to home, make a list of your favorite places to eat or visit and simply send it off in a fun email update. Consider adding it to your wedding website as well if you have one. Another creative way to do this is to set up a page on your favorite social media app that highlights all these fun places and why they are important to you as a couple. It can also be a great way of doing the things you love as a couple all over again during your engagement.

Wedding Party Appreciation Parties

Micro wedding couples take special care in selecting the right people to be in their wedding party (especially since the guest count is so small). These are the people who are there for you in times of crisis as well as times of great joy, and you'll want to show them your appreciation. Bridesmaids luncheons are quite popular and are a great way to celebrate and "shower" gifts on your bridesmaids. Traditionally there hasn't been a standard groomsmen counterpart to this party.

However, bridesmaids luncheons are not the only way to show your wedding party you appreciate them. And what about the groomsmen, "bridesdudes" (men in the bride's wedding party), and "groomsladies" (women in the groom's wedding party)? They deserve an acknowledgment too. Modern micro wedding couples are bucking the tradition of confining parties to bridesmaids. Some couples don't want to have bachelor or bachelorette parties and instead party with their attendants and show them some appreciation (whether they are all bridesmaids, groomsmen, or a mix of both). Or they host one big appreciation get-together for the attendants on both sides of the wedding party.

essential

A great gift to give your groomsmen or "bridesmen" are matching ties to go along with the wedding color palette and "tie" together the theme! Or go with something they can use again and again, like cufflinks or even some fun socks that match their individual personalities.

Again, giving your wedding party gifts is always suggested as part of the appreciation party activities. Here are some fun and meaningful ideas on how to celebrate and "shower" your wedding party with gifts and experiences:

- Host a dinner or brunch for them at your favorite restaurant or at your home.
- Go back to the Adventure and Experience Shower section in this chapter. Everything listed there can also be used as the theme of your appreciation party.
- Do something with each member of the wedding party individually or something that you know you all would love to do together as a group. Only you know what those things are.

This is a personal and meaningful way to show how much you appreciate them.

- Incorporate the appreciation for your wedding party into the entire wedding week and weekend. Treat someone (or multiple people) in your wedding party to a visit at a high-end salon for that close shave, last-minute trim, or manicure/pedicure. Take the entire wedding party out for professional massages while the two of you get a couples massage. Surprise any or all of the attendants with spa-style treatments the week of the wedding for facials, hair removal, eyebrow shaping, and more. The best thing to do is to ask each person in your wedding party what they would love the most and spoil them accordingly!

alert

Keep in mind that some people don't like to go to an abundance of parties, or may not be comfortable with certain activities. Remember, your micro wedding is about creating a meaningful experience for everyone. Always talk to your attendants first to assess their comfort level.

You get to decide what you do to say thank you to the special people in your wedding party! It is another one of the many perks of having a micro wedding.

Morning-After Brunch

If you are having a destination wedding or you're expecting a lot of guests from out of town, you should consider a brunch for the day after your wedding. Most wedding weekend brunches are held at the hotel where the majority of your guests are staying, at one of your parents' homes, or at a favorite restaurant.

> **essential**
>
> You have control over the time frame of your brunch. It can be extended to include breakfast hours, especially if you think some of your out-of-town guests might be able to join you before heading off to the airport (or hitting the road). Set your brunch at 9:00 a.m. to 1:00 p.m. if departure times differ.

This is not a mandatory event. Your wedding guests will fall into three camps:

1. Super-local guests who probably will not come to the brunch.
2. Out-of-town guests who will be exhausted and just want to get home as fast as they can and don't want to attend a brunch.
3. People who have made your wedding weekend into a longer week or weekend opportunity to explore your wonderful city or country where your destination wedding is and will likely come to brunch.

If you are aware of your guest's travel itinerary and know the majority will be sticking around (and you can afford it), then a brunch is a great idea to relax and spend more time with these loved ones.

Additional Wedding Receptions

Usually, these receptions are about celebrating your wedding in a more laid-back way and for a shorter period of time. These receptions usually last between two and five hours and almost always have a simple food and beverage menu. You can do anything from a backyard barbecue to a fun dessert and drinks reception. In the past, a fundamental reason for having a celebration like this was to include a large contingency of people who did not live anywhere near the location of your ceremony and reception venues. Otherwise, it was considered rude to invite people to another celebration of your marriage. Micro wedding planning and the COVID-19 pandemic have upended these "rules." During the mandatory quarantine of 2020, people were faced with postponing or canceling their weddings, and many decided instead to have micro weddings or multiple celebrations outside of the actual wedding day itself.

> **fact**
>
> Micro weddings were a reality prior to the pandemic and are just as popular after it. Stylish and meaningful weddings with intimate guest lists are here to stay!

This is not to say that all couples chose to have micro weddings because of COVID-19, but smaller weddings certainly became an instant reality for most worldwide throughout the pandemic.

Chapter Ten

DIY Ideas for Every Part of Your Wedding

Many couples opt to do some sort of DIY (Do-It-Yourself) project for their micro wedding. DIY wedding projects are great conversation starters and sometimes even end up being part of your home décor afterward. One very important thing to keep in mind, though, is that DIY does not necessarily mean that it will be cheaper or easier than buying something already made or custom designed by a professional. "To do or not to do" DIY is always the question, and one this chapter will help you answer.

Stationery Items and Signage

Save the Dates, invitations, signage, and other stationery items are some of the most popular things that couples end up doing DIY-style for their micro weddings. If (and only if!) you have a background in graphic design and a love for calligraphy, designing the invitations may be the best way to infuse your personality into the wedding.

---

alert

Making your own invitations is quite the task. Choosing paper size, printing, and wording is enough to drive a couple crazy. Many micro weddings are planned on an abbreviated timeline, and your invitations need to go out six to eight weeks prior.

Instead of complicating your wedding planning process, choose the right project that suits your style and set of skills.

Save the Dates

One of the easiest ways to take on some of the stationery tasks is to focus on making the Save the Date cards. Since micro weddings are often planned in a shorter period of time than larger ones, Save the Dates should be sent out as soon as possible. This is where you can use your creativity and have fun doing a DIY project without the professionals. Many Save the Dates come in postcard form or as magnets. With so many paper resources online that range from high-end premium paper to fun postcards, you can make the Save the Date an enjoyable project. And since you will be having a maximum of fifty guests, you can personalize each Save the Date.

With a postcard-style Save the Date, you can buy postcards that represent the location where you will have your wedding, especially if it is a destination event. Almost any invitation website allows you to upload your own photos onto a postcard and send them out to your guests. Magnets are another popular style for Save the Dates, as they are a great way to help remind your guests that the date is coming for your micro wedding: They can just pop the magnet right on their refrigerator, where they will see it regularly.

Many couples opt for simple email Save the Dates and use online invitation websites to ease the wedding planning process. Just note that an emailed Save the Date may be overlooked by older guests who don't have an email address (or don't check often). Be sure to check in with your older guests to see if they will have access to your virtual Save the Dates. In all likelihood, however, these older guests will be family members and will be fine without one. Consider writing them a personal note or giving them a call instead of using something online.

Invitations

If you have the skills to create your own wedding invitations, this is your chance to shine in the DIY department. If you don't have experience with designing invitations, enlist some help! If you have a particular design in mind but can't find it anywhere and don't know how to make it come to life, find a local graphic design professional or a friend who is willing to help.

> **essential**
>
> There are also tons of apps that allow you to use your phone to create interesting fonts and layouts for your invitations. Search for graphic design apps and find the one that works best for you. If you are having trouble figuring out how to print your design, research how-to instructional videos from the app designers or on *YouTube*.

If you sketch, paint, draw, or watercolor, why not make individualized invitations that suit your particular design skills? With a micro wedding, you have a small number of guests, and many of the people on your list will likely have a partner or spouse. This means you will probably not need to make fifty invitations! Most invitation companies require that you buy invitations in sets of ten or twenty-five, so using your specific skill set means that not only are you possibly saving a little money, but you can end up saving a few trees to boot.

If your guests are local and you see them often (which is more likely if they are coming to your micro wedding!), why not hand deliver these gorgeous DIY projects to as many guests as you are able? There are so many ways to personalize micro weddings, but handmade invitations are always a labor of love and your guests will know it. Hand delivering invitations to the chosen few will make them all the more special. Don't forget any of the elements you'll need for your invitations: Check back to Chapter 3!

Signage

Another element to DIY is the signage for the day of the wedding. Check back at the end of Chapter 6 for a refresher on the various popular types of signage often helpful at micro weddings. Here are some easy ways to DIY this project:

- **Welcome and ceremony signage.** The most popular ways to DIY these signs are with A-frame chalkboard displays, larger 8" × 10" frames, and wooden posts with arrows. Keep in mind that if you do design a chalkboard display, you will need to practice writing with chalk, and making a wooden post with arrows takes some carpentry skills.
- **Bar signs.** This can be as simple as printing out something pretty and sticking it in a frame or printing it on some heavy

card stock to make a tent card. Of course, if you have more advanced skills, you can create cute ways to display information about your signature cocktails and specialty beers and wines! Think about attaching the bar sign to actual wine bottles or using other glassware or tableware at the bar to display your sign.

- **Buffet and food displays.** Pretty props and printed menus in frames are always an easy way to do signage for food displays and buffets. Think about the type of food you are serving and kick up the décor a notch with props that match the theme.

- **Favor signage.** This is also easy to DIY by placing a sign in a simple frame. Be sure to get creative with the wording, describing why you chose these favors, and maybe include some extra décor props to call attention to the favors table. You'll only need signage if you are not putting favors at each place setting, or if the favors display is somehow combined with your escort cards.

- **Gift table.** While it is not proper etiquette to bring a gift to a wedding, many people do. Many guests bring envelopes with cash or checks in them. Consider having more than just a basket or a fabric box for people to place their envelopes in and a sign that says "Gifts." Think about containers you use or love in your home. Many people love using actual mailboxes, but you can get more creative than that. Have a large, gorgeous jewelry or music box? Have your guests place their gift cards inside of it. Love to garden? Go with a pretty garden-themed gift table and use a garden tool bag to collect envelopes. Love birds? Decorate the gifts table with a pretty antique birdcage. All you have to do is stick the first envelope you receive into it and no sign is needed!

- **Memory display.** This very sentimental display honors those loved ones who have passed on. Just write a clear and concise note to be placed in a frame or hung on a chair at your ceremony and keep it simple. Your loved ones would not want your wedding day to be a day of sadness but one of joy. Keeping this light and pretty is the best way to honor their memory. You can also display photos and a memory book for guests to write out special memories about those people.
- **"Guest book" display.** Why is "guest book" in quotes? In recent years, guest book displays have not been as popular as they once were traditionally. You already know who is coming to your wedding, especially when the guest list is small. However, many micro wedding couples love to get creative and interactive with their guests and opt for a unique "guest book" display. A few popular ideas include providing a Polaroid camera and having instant fun with photos. Guests can help you scrapbook them by attaching their Polaroids in a blank book and writing fun notes around them. You can also lend a time capsule feel to this "guest book" by providing pretty note cards for guests to write their well wishes for you as newlyweds or offer their advice for a long-lasting marriage. Guests will then place the notes in a nice container or vase of your choosing. Something like this will require a sign explaining what your guests are to do. Find some colorful pens to go along with it and pop that sign in a pretty frame!

Other Stationery Items

A few other possible stationery items that you might want to DIY for your micro wedding day are programs, escort and place cards, and menus.

- **Programs and menus.** One of the simplest ways to make programs and menus is by printing out a design that you have created either on an app or with a specific software you have (like PowerPoint, Canva, Adobe InDesign, etc.) and taking it to a shop that provides copy and print services. A printshop can copy your design right onto heavy card stock and cut them to the dimensions you want. Some home printers can handle card stock as well; all you will need to do is buy a paper cutter!
- **Escort cards and place cards.** Find your desired style of cards either in a local stationery store or online. It is easy to find tent cards and business-sized cards in various colors to match your color palette. If you want to write these out yourself, try your hand at calligraphy or simply use your own nice handwriting. Some invitation stores (both brick-and-mortar and online) can also print these for you.

Flowers and Décor

Flowers and other types of décor aren't usually high on the DIY list for many couples. Décor like escort card displays, menus, programs, and family picture displays are the easiest DIY projects for a micro wedding. Flowers, on the other hand, are not the easiest to handle yourself, no matter how small the wedding is.

Floral design takes practice, but you may have a knack for it. Or maybe your mom wants to make your bridal bouquet from the garden you and she built together in your childhood backyard. Perhaps a friend is known for their flower arrangements and is willing to help out. Regardless, be sure you understand the logistics of taking on floral designs for your wedding day. A bridal bouquet is one thing, but taking care of the bridesmaids' bouquets, boutonnieres, altar arrangements, trellis design, centerpieces, cake flowers, cocktail tables, and so on is a whole other ballgame. There are florists, and then there are *wedding* florists. Wedding florists focus on weddings and events only and will pay more attention to the details of the day as opposed to just creating florals that look like everyday deliveries. Flowers come in various quantities when you purchase them, and are typically not groomed for you (meaning thorns are not removed, stems are not cut at certain angles, foliage is not removed from stems). You really should not buy your wedding flowers any time earlier than two days prior to your wedding, either, if you do not have proper refrigeration for them. The last thing you want is for delicate flowers to die before your wedding day. You'll need to design and pack them for transport and find people to take them and set them up at your venue(s).

---

alert

Even if you can transport and store all the flowers you'll need, consider whether this is something you really want to do. You will be very busy getting ready to be married; be sure not to overload yourself with tasks you can delegate to others or have a professional do unless you are truly excited about doing them yourself.

Transportation for flowers (and other décor) is something that most couples do not think about, but it must be addressed when planning your micro wedding. If you have fifty guests, you will need anywhere from five to twelve centerpieces, depending on the number and size of your tables. You may also need cocktail table arrangements. Then there are the ceremony arrangements with personal flowers, altar arrangements, and any welcome arrangements and aisle décor. Make sure you have a big enough vehicle to transport these items, or that anyone you delegate transportation to has a large enough vehicle and is aware of the time frame that is allowed by your ceremony and reception sites for décor delivery. This person should not be a member of the wedding party, as they will need to place the flowers on the tables once the caterers have set up the linens, and your attendants will be busy getting themselves ready. Someone will need to break down all of these floral décor items after the wedding and transport them from the venue(s) as well.

fact

Most reception sites and hotels don't allow for early delivery of flowers. The delivery window is usually about two hours prior to the reception time (not the ceremony time) unless your ceremony is in the same location. Then you have about one hour afterward to break down your décor.

With a micro wedding, your guest list could have fewer than fifteen people, making this an easier DIY. You may also want a few simpler florals versus a bigger range, depending on the style of your wedding. Maybe you end up putting your bridal bouquet in a vase at the reception, where you have just one table for ten. Easy! You are the judge of the floral needs for your micro wedding. You know the look you want and your budget.

Here are a few easy suggestions for going DIY with floral designs:

- Use dried florals and place them in smaller vases ahead of time to place in the bathroom, welcome tables, gift tables, mantels, and other small places like end tables and furniture vignettes. Dried lavender and eucalyptus smell great even when they are dried, and you can apply lavender or eucalyptus oils to them to revive their scent even further.
- Grab some roses from your local grocery store for the petals that your flower girl will throw or for the petals for your aisle or for décor underneath your mandap (for Hindu ceremonies).
- Keep it simple for bouquets by grabbing one type of flower and tying them in a small bunch if you are on a tighter budget and have the time to do this (and the space for bringing them with you).
- Go with simple greenery around the base of small lanterns or a small bunch of pillar and votive candles for your centerpieces (be sure you have another person to place the centerpieces for you).
- Instead of flowers, use fruits and arrange them in bowls for centerpieces. If you are having a tropical or beach theme, paint a few pineapples with the color palette of your wedding and place them on your cocktail tables or on your escort card table.

To help you prepare for your floral design needs, check out the Floral Design Worksheet in the Appendix.

Food and Drinks

Food and drinks are two of the trickier wedding elements to take care of from a DIY perspective. Many venues will not allow you to provide your own catering, but some will allow you to provide dessert and alcohol. (This is something you will have considered when choosing your venue; take another look at the information on food and beverages at wedding venues in Chapter 4.) If you are not having your micro wedding at a hotel (most hotels forbid bringing in your own alcohol), find out if you can purchase your own alcohol to bring in and maybe choose a fun signature cocktail that you can premix for your micro wedding day.

> **essential**
>
> When it comes to food prepping, consider how many guests you're inviting. A dinner for ten is considerably easier than a dinner for fifty. Be aware of your limitations and what things you really want to do yourself versus delegate to someone else.

If it is just the two of you self-officiating or just your immediate family in attendance, why not have a family-style meal at someone's home instead of at a wedding venue? You can even have a mix of food styles when you are having a small home wedding. If you and your fiancé adore the taco place down the street, have them provide a taco station while you put together a fun charcuterie display with your own fancy wooden boards or that three-tiered tray you have been dying to buy at the local antique store (it could become a family heirloom)! Even if you are a chef, you may not want to cook on your wedding day, but you might have friends willing to help out. Maybe you have a friend who is a chef too or loves to cook, for example.

If you do decide to take care of the food prep for your wedding day, be sure you have a lot of help serving the food. There are caterers and waitstaff companies in most metropolitan areas that can take care of the setup, service, and cleanup without providing the actual food. A quick *Google* search or call to a few caterers should be helpful in finding the service you need.

One of the easiest ways to incorporate your own style into the food element of your micro wedding is with desserts! Who says you have to have a super-expensive wedding cake? What if you love chocolate? Or waffles? Or ice cream? The best way to DIY your wedding day dessert is simply to serve your favorite desserts in the way you eat them at home. Have a waffle bar with a toaster, waffles straight from the frozen food section, and a bunch of pretty bowls with a variety of fruits and other toppings like whipped cream and local syrups to delight your guests with. Maybe bring out your grandmother's china for this. Or you can go to the local thrift store and pick out a fun array of antique plates if you are going for a shabby-chic vibe. Desserts don't ever have to be fussy and should be fun! If you and your fiancé love doughnuts, DIY a fun display and have your friend or your planner pick up a variety of doughnuts from your favorite vendor on the way to the wedding (if they don't deliver). If you love cake, why not bake a few of your favorite cakes or ask a couple talented friends to make cakes? The dessert DIY options for micro weddings are myriad, and you should absolutely have your favorite dessert at your wedding.

Consider taking care of the beverages as well as (or instead of) handling the food. A great way to incorporate your own style is to provide some of your local favorite sodas or beers. Or, if you have your own soda maker, whip up something special for the big day! Are you a microbrewer? Why not make a signature beer for your own wedding? And if you love to concoct delicious cocktails, your guests will surely know it and will enjoy seeing a little of that flair at your wedding.

Finally, when it comes to going DIY for any food or beverage element, always keep safety in mind. Wash your hands before handling any food. Using food-safe gloves and face masks is an extra step that many of your guests will appreciate. The last thing you want to do is have your guests get sick because of what you decided to do from a DIY perspective. There are reasons why caterers, hotels, and restaurants have licenses and large insurance policies.

DIY Bar

Setting up your own bar requires more than just liquor. You'll need garnishes, like maraschino cherries, lemons, limes, celery, and olives. Be sure to stock mixers, like soft drinks, club soda, tonic water, still and sparkling water, and juices. You'll need ice, swizzle sticks, and cocktail napkins. Now for the hard stuff: beer, wine, and liquor. If you are concerned about guests having too much to drink, here's a tip: Don't serve salty foods. They only make people thirstier. Do serve meats, fish, cheese, and other high-protein foods. They restore blood sugar, which is depleted when someone drinks alcohol, and they help sober up guests who have had too much. Coffee will only wind up a drunk person; it won't sober them up. Provide plenty of water as well to flush out their systems. There is always the option of providing transportation with a shuttle for all of your guests and having taxis or rideshare services available.

The most common question couples have when setting up a DIY bar is how much alcohol to buy. The best advice is to always buy a little more than you think you will need. You definitely don't want to run out of alcohol in the middle of the reception. Remember from Chapter 7 that most liquor stores will let you return any unopened bottles of alcohol (but you will not be able to return anything that has been chilled).

On average, for an evening reception serving fifty guests a two- to three-course meal, you will need the following for a full bar and dinner:*

- Champagne or sparkling wine for a toast: 9–10 bottles, depending on the number of guests (most bottles provide 5–6 glasses each)
- Red wine: 5 bottles (just for the bar; this will increase if you want multiple types)
- White wine: 9 bottles (just for the bar; this will increase if you want multiple types)
- Beer: 2 cases
- Whiskey: 1 liter
- Bourbon: 1 liter
- Gin: 1 liter
- Scotch: 1–2 liters (This amount will depend heavily on your crowd and if you know they like scotch)
- Rum: 1 liter
- Vodka: 3 liters
- Tequila: 1 liter
- Dry vermouth: 1 bottle
- Sweet vermouth: 1 bottle
- Tonic: 1 case
- Club soda: 1 case

- Cranberry juice: 1–2 gallons
- Orange juice: 1–2 gallons
- Grapefruit juice: 1–2 gallons
- Wine with dinner: There are approximately 4–6 glasses per bottle and you will need 2 glasses per person (or more or less, depending on how much different guests tend to drink) throughout a three-course meal. You will want both red and white wine handy, and your caterer might suggest specific types of wine for each course. Obviously, the amount of wine and the types of wine will increase with the number of courses you will be having.

This list will change if you are providing only beer and wine. See the Appendix for more information on how to prepare a beer and wine bar.

When it comes to bar equipment rentals, you will need to know your crowd. Think about an average of four to five drinks per person. Some basic rental equipment you will need are water goblets/glasses, highball and rocks glasses, wineglasses, and champagne flutes, in addition to the garnishes, mixers, ice, swizzle sticks, and cocktail napkins mentioned previously. You may also need martini glasses if you plan on serving martinis and/or cosmos. You need a way to mix drinks, such as cocktail shakers, and have containers or glasses to store your garnishes in. In terms of ice, you'll need enough not only for the drinks themselves, but to keep the beer and wine cold. Don't forget receptacles for the ice—separate ones for ice that will be added to drinks and ice that is to chill beer and wine. If you plan on serving margaritas and piña coladas, then you need more ice for blending, coconut milk, salt(s), and blenders. Ask your caterer or the rental company for some advice on quantities for all of these items. Remember, caterers do this every day and will be able to give you averages based on the age groups and number of guests.

Vows

Your vows are the perfect place to go DIY for your micro wedding. Writing your own vows will give the ceremony a personal DIY twist instead of just repeating what your officiant says.

A micro wedding has fewer guests, and the likelihood is that they will be paying closer attention to what you say at the ceremony than, say, a mass with two hundred guests. The ceremony will probably be shorter, and you will be surrounded by those you love the most. Your vows will have more meaning in this intimate setting, so take the time to write them yourself (and enlist the help of your officiant when needed).

When writing your vows, focus on whether you want to keep it short and sweet or go into more depth about how you fell in love. If you choose something more detailed, remember that this is not the time to talk about anything embarrassing, like when your partner had a stomach virus on your second date and threw up all over your couch. Your wedding vows are something that you want to remember fondly—not something that makes you cringe when you think back to them.

The process for writing very personal vows can feel a little daunting at first, but if you focus on three main reasons why you fell in love with this person, it can help keep things to the point, ensuring a memorable speech that your guests will pay attention to. Include a short story to illustrate each of the three reasons.

The next step is to convey the promises (or key vows) you will keep in your marriage and that you know are important to your fiancé. Write them in a way that will be easy for you to remember. Color, taste, sound, and smell all factor into memory and attaching a sensory detail to the promises can help you remember. Attach the promise in your mind to a visualization of your fiancé, along with one other sensory detail to help you remember.

Your vows should be written down in physical form and kept after the wedding. To have a meaningful micro wedding is to have a meaningful ceremony, and vows play an essential role in this rite of passage. Don't just log them in your mind to be forgotten after the ceremony, or bullet the main points on a note in your phone to delete later.

Although your vows are a serious part of the ceremony, it does not mean that you can't be funny, romantic, and silly. It just means these are vows and they are important! It is imperative that what you say emphasizes togetherness and being there for each other during good and difficult times (as hard times come for all of us). Use your own language and focus only on what your partner will enjoy hearing, not what everyone else expects. Think of your vows as the showcase of the deepest feelings you have for each other.

Finally, you will need to end your vows with an "everlasting" statement. What does that mean? It points to how you will be together from this point on. It's the "until death do us part" moment. You don't have to use those words exactly, as this is part of the DIY element and you probably don't use this out-of-the-ordinary language in your daily life, but do make a point of conveying that your commitment is forever.

---

essential

Here's a quick checklist for writing your vows:
- ❏ Always start your vows with three positive reasons why you are marrying your fiancé.
- ❏ Add stories behind your reasons to keep it meaningful.
- ❏ Lay out specific promises that you intend to keep throughout your marriage.
- ❏ End the vows with an "everlasting" statement of how you will be together until the end.

Because this is a super-important part of your ceremony, don't wait until the last minute to start writing. Don't feel like you need to write it all at once, either. It's best to just write a little bit at a time beginning at the start of your wedding planning so you can mull over each element over time. It will help the vows to feel "just right" and meaningful on the wedding day.

One great way to keep the pressure off and to feel like you are on the right track is to get an idea of what your partner is writing. Remember, you are getting married, so writing your vows together is perfectly okay. You don't have to keep them a secret from each other, and you can work through them together if you like. If you and/or your partner are running in circles about what to say, here are some questions to ask yourselves to jump-start your creative writing juices:

- When was the day you knew that you wanted to marry your partner?
- How is your life different with your partner?
- What were you lacking in your life before they entered it?
- How has your partner changed you for the better?
- Has that person gotten you through something really difficult?
- What do you miss the most about your partner when they are not around?
- What would you do to make sure that person is happy and healthy?

Always remember that in the end, your vows are about how you will keep your love like the burning flame it is right now! Communication is key in a healthy marriage, and your vows are a wonderful way of communicating your promises of love to each other.

Music

Music is another part of the micro wedding where couples like to add a DIY touch. As it is the number one form of entertainment at the event, be sure to think through your options and the pros and cons of where to use professionals. If you have close to fifty guests coming to your wedding, you may want to think about having a DJ or a band for the reception and focus on having the DIY music portion at your ceremony. The more wedding guests you have, the more complicated the reception gets. Leave the complications to a professional.

Some couples include a DIY musical element by enlisting the help of family or friends who have musical talent. For example, if your best friend is an amazing cellist, why not have them play a lovely musical prelude, or even the music for the entire ceremony? If you are not having attendants, this is a great way to include someone close to you in your wedding party. And if you or your fiancé plays an instrument, sings, is a DJ, or is in a band, only you know how you will incorporate your talents on your wedding day. For example, if you want to sing a song, maybe consider singing while there is a natural break in the timeline of the day. A few great time frames are right after the welcome toast, during the cake cutting, or while your band is taking a break. If your partner would love to perform with the band, allocate a short block of time for them to join in. Just be sure you or your partner is not taking on too much of the music tasks as you want to be able to enjoy your wedding day together.

> **fact**
>
> When it comes to doing the music yourself, keep it simple so you can truly enjoy the day. You want to remember the music as a fun experience as opposed to a chore.

If you are having a wedding in a private home, it should be easy enough to put a playlist together and play it through your sound system for the ceremony and the reception if you choose. However, keep in mind that there is a reason why there are DJs and bands at most weddings. Music is a big part of the atmosphere of your wedding, and as the night goes on and the liquor is flowing, the task of running music and keeping your guests dancing can become a tiring one if you are actually trying to enjoy yourself (which you should be). Enlisting your friends for this job carries the same caveat—you want them to enjoy themselves too. So, think about the level of entertainment you want at your wedding (a mix of different genres; stopping for first dances, father-daughter dances, etc.; an introduction to the reception for you and your new spouse) and how much of this you truly want to DIY.

Photography

While photography is not a common DIY element at weddings (as any professional can tell you, there are a number of factors involved in executing great photos with minimal stress), it is possible when you enlist friends and family to help. If photos are straining your budget, one way to DIY is to think through your guest list (or people who did not make the guest list but are dear friends of yours). Do any of them have a camera and a little photography skill? Do you know anyone who does photojournalism (works for a local newspaper)? Do you live near a school where college students take photography classes (most community colleges have them)? Use these resources!

If none of these are possible, consider hiring a professional wedding photographer on an hourly basis. Most photographers have packages with coverages anywhere from six to ten hours;

however, some offer their services by the hour with minimums (like three to five hours). This may be harder to find in larger metropolitan cities but easier in suburban or rural locations, where there are likely more independent photographers with less rigid contracts. If you do find a professional who agrees to an hourly rate, you will need at least three hours of coverage to ensure you get photos from the most important parts of the day. Beyond the ceremony and any portraits you want, make sure the photographer covers your "getting ready" time frame. Some of the more important details you will want to photograph include:

- What the two of you are wearing
- Your engagement rings and wedding bands, along with any other interesting jewelry
- Whoever is helping you/your partner into your/their dress
- Tying your tie/your partner tying their tie
- Your bouquets and boutonnieres
- The wedding invitations

Many professional wedding photographers will use flat lay photography to help focus on some of the smaller details. Make sure you have a succinct list of what you want ahead of time so the photographer can check them off as they go.

> **question**
>
> **What is a "flat lay" in terms of wedding photography?**
> A flat lay is where the photographer will literally lay your detailed personal items from your wedding day on the ground or in a beautiful setting (or specialty flat lay boards) and take "aerial" shots and close-ups of them for "Instagrammable" stylistic photos.

Remember, you have limited time with your photographer in an hourly contract, and they will most certainly charge you for any extra time. Be concise and enlist the help of your wedding party and family ahead of time to make sure everyone is where they are supposed to be when the time comes for photos to be taken. Then, enlist one of your guests who is good at taking nice, clear photos on their cell phone to photograph your toasts, cake cutting, and first dances (and any other details you want reminders of after the wedding is over). However, in large metropolitan cities, you are likely to find young and hungry creatives who would be more than happy to try their skills at your wedding for less money. Just be sure they have some sort of photography examples to show you how creative they are.

> **fact**
>
> Many engaged couples use HoneyFund.com as their gift registry to put toward their honeymoon. However, you can use this website for anything you are saving up for. Photography is certainly something you can save for, especially when it comes to the final payment!

The main takeaway here is that you should not take photography for granted. Photographers are expensive because they are worth it. You will be grateful in the end if you can have a professional for at least part of your day. It might not hurt to ask all your family members for this one gift of helping you pay for the photographer.

Wedding Planning Checklists

While planning your micro wedding, the following checklists can help keep you on track throughout the process. Here you will find help for creating your budget, wording invitations correctly, considering catering options, and more. Each checklist includes information on the chapter you can refer to for more information about the checklist topic.

Budgeting Your Micro Wedding (Chapter 2)

It is important to realize that your wedding budget is not going to fit into the box of "average wedding" budgets. Most national and international wedding websites and "authorities" base their percentages on weddings that average between 100 and 150 guests. This does not mean a simple and easy percentage calculation across the board for you.

Start with the first line in this table as your base budget—how much you ultimately want to spend (or not exceed). Then calculate each row as a percentage of that number and enter the dollar amount in the right-most column. The first five lines of this budget spreadsheet are "optional" in the sense of including them in your actual wedding day budget. Most of them are seen as investments. Many couples teeter back and forth as to whether or not a wedding planner or designer is an investment or part of the wedding day budget. Most planners—even "Day of" coordinators—work with you and handle all sorts of things for you far in advance of the wedding day.

Estimated Budget			$
Wedding Element	**Estimated Amount**	**Notes/Discount Possibilities**	**Actual Cost**
Wedding Planner or Designer	10% of your budget	This can also be seen as investment.	$
Wedding Dress & Accessories	Investment	Remember that these may be mementos or can be sold afterward.	$
Suits & Accessories	Investment	Remember that these may be mementos or can be sold afterward.	$
Rings	Investment	You will have these for the rest of your life.	$
Wedding Insurance	Investment	This can be done through your renter's or homeowner's insurance. There are also specific wedding insurance companies.	$
Catering/Desserts/ Rentals/Staffing	40%–60% of your budget	The range can be broad due to the smaller guest count and your desires.	$
Flowers	7%–15% of your budget	The range can be broad due to the smaller guest count and your desires.	$
Invitations/ Stationery	0%–3% of your budget	Depends on the formality of your wedding. Ranges anywhere from an informal email to printed invitations.	$

Music	5%–8% of your budget	Depends on whether or not you are having a band or DJ.	$
Venue Rental	0%–10% of your budget	This amount varies widely, as the wedding can be at your home without a tent or at a reduced rate for timing purposes.	$
Officiant/Church	0%–1% of your budget	Self-officiating vs. having a friend do this vs. place of worship officiants.	$
Photography	10% of your budget	Never spend less than this. Photography is what you are left with after the wedding.	$
Videography	0%–10% of your budget	Approximately 44% of couples hire a videographer. Definitely worth it, but many see it as a luxury.	$
Beauty	2%–5% of your budget	Depends on whether or not you pay for your attendants/moms.	$
Favors	0%–3% of your budget	Some couples don't offer favors, and some do.	$
Shuttles/Transportation	0%–5% of your budget	This ultimately depends on your guest list and their needs.	$
Misc.			$
Total Actual Cost			**$**

Invitation and Insert Wording (Chapter 3)

After reading Chapter 3, you may need a little more help on how to word your invitations in certain circumstances. All invitations and their inserts need to be written carefully. It is absolutely imperative that you have at least three pairs of eyes to look over all wording for every element of your invitation. The last thing you want is to realize after you send the invitations that you spelled your last name wrong because you didn't have someone proofread!

When the bride and groom host their own wedding:

The honor of your presence is requested
at the marriage of
Miss Elizabeth Elaine Parker
and
Mr. Justin Clark

Miss Elizabeth Elaine Parker
and
Mr. Justin James Clark
request the honor of your presence
at their marriage

When the bride's parents host the wedding:

Mr. and Mrs. Roger Parker
request the honor of your presence
at the marriage of their daughter
Elizabeth Elaine
to
Mr. Justin Clark
on Saturday, the seventh of August,
Two thousand twenty-one
at two o'clock in the afternoon
Fairview Baptist Church
Fairview, Pennsylvania

When the groom's parents host the wedding:

Mr. and Mrs. Robert Clark
request the honor of your presence
at the marriage of
Miss Elizabeth Elaine Parker
to their son
Mr. Justin James Clark
on Saturday, the seventh of August,
Two thousand twenty-one
at two o'clock in the afternoon
Fairview Baptist Church
Fairview, Pennsylvania

When both the bride's and groom's parents host the wedding:

Mr. and Mrs. Roger Parker
and
Mr. and Mrs. Robert Clark
request the honor of your presence
at the marriage of their children
Elizabeth Elaine
and
Justin James
on Saturday, the seventh of August,
Two thousand twenty-one
at two o'clock in the afternoon
Fairview Baptist Church
Fairview, Pennsylvania

Mr. and Mrs. Roger Parker
request the honor of your presence
at the marriage of their daughter
Elizabeth Elaine Parker
to
Justin James Clark
son of Mr. and Mrs. Robert Clark
Saturday, the seventh of August,
Two thousand twenty-one
at two o'clock in the afternoon
Fairview Baptist Church
Fairview, Pennsylvania

Divorced Hosts

Circumstances will vary when divorced parents host a wedding. Use these examples as general guidelines.

When the mother of the bride is hosting and is not remarried:

*Mrs. James Parker
requests the honor of your presence
at the marriage of her daughter
Elizabeth Elaine*

When the father of the bride is hosting and is not remarried:

*Mr. Roger Parker
requests the honor of your presence
at the marriage of his daughter
Elizabeth Elaine*

When the mother of the bride is hosting and has remarried:

*Mrs. David C. Hayes
requests the honor of your presence
at the marriage of her daughter
Elizabeth Elaine Parker*

*Mr. and Mrs. David C. Hayes
request the honor of your presence
at the marriage of Mrs. Hayes's
daughter
Elizabeth Elaine Parker*

When the father of the bride is hosting and has remarried:

*Mr. and Mrs. Roger Parker
request the honor of your presence
at the marriage of Mr. Parker's
daughter
Elizabeth Elaine*

Deceased Parents

Deceased parents are usually not mentioned on wedding invitations because only the hosts of the event are listed. However, if you want to mention your late mother or father, no one is going to fault you for it.

When one parent is deceased and the host has not remarried:

Mrs. Ann Parker
requests the honor of your presence
at the marriage of
Elizabeth Elaine,
daughter of Mrs. Parker and the late
Roger Parker

When both parents are deceased, a close friend or relative may host:

Mr. and Mrs. Frederick Parker
request the honor of your presence
at the marriage of their
granddaughter
Elizabeth Elaine Parker

When one parent is deceased and the host has remarried:

Mr. and Mrs. David Spencer
request the honor of your presence
at the marriage of Mrs. Spencer's
daughter
Elizabeth Elaine

Military Ceremonies

In military weddings, rank determines the placement of names. If the person's rank is lower than sergeant, omit the rank, but list their branch of service. Junior officers' titles are placed below their names, followed by their branches of service. Titles are placed before names if the rank is higher than lieutenant, followed by their branches of service on the next line.

When the person's rank is lower than sergeant:

Mr. and Mrs. Roger Parker
request the honor of your presence
at the marriage of their daughter
Beth Elaine
United States Army
to
Justin James Clark

When the person's rank is higher than lieutenant:

Mr. and Mrs. Roger Parker
request the honor of your presence
at the marriage of their daughter
Beth Elaine
to
Captain Justin James Clark
United States Navy

When the person has a junior officer's title:

Mr. and Mrs. Roger Parker
request the honor of your presence
at the marriage of their daughter
Beth Elaine
to
Justin James Clark
First Lieutenant, United States Navy

Catering Checklist (Chapter 7)

The most important decisions you will make for your wedding day in terms of budget are your catering and rental aspects. This will be anywhere from 40 percent to 60 percent of your budget for a micro wedding. The following list of questions for your catering selection process will help you gather all the information you need to make this important decision during your wedding planning process.

- What is their average price range? Do they have printed price sheets?

- Will they do rentals on your behalf?

- Do they provide specialty menus, or do they only have set menus?

- Are prices dependent on the foods chosen, or is there an all-inclusive rate?

- How many waiters per person? What will they wear?

- Do they charge a gratuity rate? What rate is it?

- Do they have another event that weekend? At the same venue? How many weddings does your sales rep take, on average, per weekend? If more than two, do they have assistants to help them? What are their names and contact information?

- Do they have a list of references?

- How do they serve the coffee and tea?

- What types of wait service do they provide—plated, buffet, family style, French, Russian, or other?

- Can you provide a special recipe for them to reproduce?

- Do they have a license? Insurance?

- Do they have menus for vegans/vegetarians, gluten-free/celiac guests, people with peanut allergies and other major allergies, diabetic options, low-fat, kosher, halal, or other dietary needs?

- Can they provide the alcohol? How many bartenders will they have? Is there a corkage fee? Can special requests be made for certain types of liquor and special glassware? How do they price these differences?

- How will the food be displayed on the buffet?

- Do they provide wedding cakes or desserts?

- Is there a cake-cutting fee for an outside cake provider?

- Do they have a setup with local community kitchens to take any leftover food?

- Will they provide a going-away box for the couple at the end of the reception?

- Who is the contact person?

- What is their retainer/deposit policy? Is it refundable or nonrefundable?

- What is their postponement policy?

- What are their safety protocols?

- Do they recycle or compost?

Floral Design Worksheet (Chapters 6 and 10)

Most couples want some sort of floral designs for their micro wedding. This worksheet will help you plan what your needs are in relation to your ceremony and reception venue(s) before you meet with your florist. This worksheet can also help you if you decide to try a DIY approach to floral design for your micro wedding day.

Item Needed	Description	Quantity	Cost per Item
Bridal Bouquet(s)			
Toss Bouquet(s)			
Headpiece/Hair Flowers			
Bridesmaids/MOH/ Bridesmen			
Bridesmaids/MOH Hair Flowers			
Flower Girl Hair Flowers			
Flower Girl Hair Wreaths			

Item Needed	Description	Quantity	Cost per Item
Flower Girl Basket(s) and Petals			
Flower Girl Pomander(s)			
Flower Girl Garland/Other Décor			
Sisters(s)' Corsages (Pin-on or Wrist)			
Mothers' Corsages (Pin-on or Wrist)			
Grandmothers' Corsages (Pin-on or Wrist)			
Mothers' or Grandmothers' Nosegay(s)			
Female Officiant(s)			
Female Reader(s)			
Female Musician(s) or Vocalist(s)			

Item Needed	Description	Quantity	Cost per Item
Groom(s)			
Groomsmen/Best Man/Groomsladies Attendants			
Ring Bearer Boutonniere(s)			
Ring Bearer Pillow(s) or Box(es)			
Brother(s)' Boutonniere(s)			
Fathers' Boutonnieres			
Grandfathers' Boutonnieres			
Ushers' Boutonnieres			
Male Officiant(s)			
Male Reader(s)			

Item Needed	Description	Quantity	Cost per Item
Male Musician(s) or Vocalist(s)			
Other Personal Flowers Needed			
Ceremony Altar Décor			
Pedestals			
Aisle Décor			
Aisle Runner			
Garland(s) for Structures			
Potted Flowers			
Potted Plants			
Lighting			

Item Needed	Description	Quantity	Cost per Item
Candle Holders/ Lanterns			
Ceremonial Décor for Religious Purposes			
Wreaths			
Other Ceremony Décor Needed			
Cocktail Table Flowers or Candles			
Escort Card Display			
Gift/Card Display/ Box/Basket			
Memory Table Display			
Entrance/Welcome Décor			
Garlands for Staircases/Mantels/ Doorways/etc.			

Item Needed	Description	Quantity	Cost per Item
Candles and Candle Holders for Reception			
Centerpiece(s)			
Cake Flowers and Décor			
Guest Book or Memory Table			
Tent Décor			
Lighting			
Other Reception Décor Needed			

Beer and Wine–Only Bar Checklist (Chapter 7)

The most important thing to think about when having only beer and wine (in terms of alcoholic beverages) at your bar (and for dinner) is your guest list. You will need to make assumptions about certain guests as to whether or not they are teetotalers, light drinkers, average drinkers, or heavy drinkers. This checklist assumes the following:*

- You will have fifty guests.
- You will have a cocktail hour and a four-hour reception.
- Ten of your guests will be light drinkers, consuming an average of one to two alcoholic beverages (or won't drink alcohol at all).
- Thirty-five of your guests will be average drinkers, consuming approximately three to five alcoholic beverages.
- Five of your guests will be heavy drinkers, consuming more than five drinks.

It is always best to round up if you are not sure.

Keep in mind that this checklist is based on you providing your own beer and wine for the reception. Wherever you purchase your alcohol, find out if you can return any of it. In most major cities, purveyors will allow you to return unchilled and unopened beer and wine. Research everything first and ask your caterer, wedding planner, newlyweds, venues, and trusted friends for advice on the best place to find beer and wine for your wedding. If returns are possible, always buy more than you think you need so you don't have to make a "beer run" in the middle of your wedding reception.

Beer

You will need at least six cases of beer (for fifty guests). If you are having specialty and local beers, you may want to add one to two cases of each type of beer in case your guests really end up liking one over the other. You should, in general, offer at least three types of beer. With smaller weddings, the fewer guests you have, the easier it is to find out ahead of time what types of beer they like (or don't like). Lagers and ales are the safest choices in general. European and US-brand lagers are typical at American weddings, as are pale and dark ales. Pale ales, India pale ales (IPAs), and stouts are the most popular ales at weddings.

Wine

You should have no less than three cases of wine at your wedding (for fifty guests). If you know your guest list will barely drink beer and will focus more on wine, you should double the amount of wine. This is where the pricing will have the broadest range. Wines differ in pricing all over the world. You will need wine at the bar and wine for dinner if you are having a seated affair. Usually the more popular varietals like merlot, pinot noir, cabernet sauvignon, malbec, pinot grigio, chardonnay, and sauvignon blanc are offered at the bar. For a catered seated dinner, ask your caterer for suggestions on what types of wine pair best with each course you are serving. At a less formal event, be sure to have (at the very least) two types of red and two types of white wine.

Index

About the Author

Katie Martin is a world-renowned author, wedding expert, speaker, wedding planner, and floral designer based in the Washington, DC, metropolitan area. Her work has been featured in *The Washington Post*, blogs, social media, magazines, and museum exhibits, as well as on CNN, NBC, CBS, ABC, and TLC. She has planned and designed more than 3,500 weddings in more than thirty different countries. She is also the author of *The Everything® Wedding Book*, 4th and 5th editions; *The Everything® Mother of the Bride Book*, 2nd, 3rd, and 4th editions; and *The Mother of the Bride Guide: A Modern Mom's Guide to Wedding Planning*, along with countless print and online wedding expert articles. Learn more about her and her team at EleganceandSimplicity.com or on her social media accounts at @eleganceandsimplicityinc.